A Scientific Approach

To

Biblical Mysteries

A Scientific Approach

To

Biblical Mysteries

Robert W. Faid

New Leaf Press

First Printing: June 1993
Second Printing: October 1993
Third Printing: April 1994

Library of Congress Catalog Number: 92-85131
ISBN: 0-89221-231-4

All Scripture in this book is from the King James Version of the
Bible.

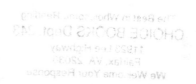

This book is dedicated to
my mother-in-law,
Freda E. Winslow,
A true handmaiden of our Lord.

And to my uncles,
Vernon M. Faid,
One of God's real Olympic champions.
And
Arthur J. Faid,
Who has quietly done so much for so many,
And asked for little in return.

The problem with reading Robert Faid's books is that your gut keeps saying "Yes," but your mind goes, "Now just a cotton picking minute here."

People who have spent a lifetime resisting their gut reaction will find this book very disturbing.

— Ben Kinchlow
Co-host, The 700 Club

What a fascinating and delightful book! Reads like a fiction thriller, yet it is based on facts and logic. Robert Faid takes the armchair traveler on a marvelous journey of discovery into the very heart of the Bible, unraveling the most wonderful mysteries, and unlocking secret after secret along the way. A SCIENTIFIC AP-PROACH TO BIBLICAL MYSTERIES truly reveals the glory of God. I most highly recommend this superb book.

— Texe Marrs
President, Living Truth Ministries
Best-selling author

It isn't simply its logic, scientific perception, or clarity of thought that makes A SCIENTIFIC APPROACH TO BIBLICAL MYSTER-IES an effective tool for witnessing. It's the author's love for Jesus smiling from every page. Such love is irresistible to the lost but thirsting soul.

Beyond that, this book is a "time-out" for the battle-worn soldier of the Cross. Each chapter is an oasis, a cool and refreshing way to replenish your resolve and fortify your faith. Drink from this book often. Your esteem for God's Word will thrive as never before.

— Rev. David A. Ingraham
Southwest Radio Church

Contents

Preface

The Bible is the most fascinating book ever written — or that ever *could* be written. It is more of a library than a single book, with sixty-six volumes attributed to about fifty authors separated in time by perhaps fifteen hundred years. Yet there is a continuity of theme throughout: the revelation of God, the Creator — to His creation — man.

In it is history and geography, the greatest and most intense stories of love and success, and of dismal failure and utter destruction. It foretells the rise of mighty empires and their rulers, and their demise and eventual downfall. It tells us of both unbelievable wealth and of the most abject poverty. In it is found goodness and mercy as well as vileness and evil. The Bible touches on every possible aspect of human life and the supreme holiness of God. In it is *everything!*

But it also contains mysteries!

How, for example, did Moses know what happened in the Garden of Eden? And did a man and a woman named Adam and Eve really live at all, or is this just a symbolic representation of our early ancestors? Exactly when was Jesus born? Was there really a Star of Bethlehem? Can there actually be *physical* places the Bible calls heaven and hell? Can we really believe that impossible story of the sun moving *backward*? And what about Jonah? Was it possible that a big fish could actually swallow him — and he lived to tell about the experience? These are just a few of the mysteries that have caused some people *not* to take the Bible seriously.

I am convinced that what the Bible tells us is true. This book is an attempt to answer some of the questions which biblical critics have raised and to give possible scientific explanations for events which scoffers call "impossible."

Christians can never effectively witness to unbelievers

when they cannot respond to those who question the Bible's accuracy. Herman Bailey, host of the nationally televised Christian program "Action Sixties," remarked to me recently, "A Christian should not be like an ostrich with his head buried in the sand. He has to know the answers to the hard questions unbelievers will ask."

You certainly won't find the answer to everything in this book, but I hope that you will find it enjoyable, interesting, and informative for yourself, and that it will enable you to better witness to those who have not yet discovered that in Jesus Christ they *will* find the ultimate answer in their lives — now and for eternity.

1

The Genesis Account! Was It Recorded by Eyewitnesses?

Whenever I read the Book of Genesis, I have a deep and almost overwhelming emotional and spiritual experience. In the first chapter it is as though I am an eyewitness to creation, standing upon the summit of a high mountain peak and watching these primordial events happening before my very eyes.

These plain and straightforward passages are the epitome of brevity and condensation, for in a scant thirty-one verses the entire history of the creation of the earth and all that lives upon it is revealed. There is not one excess word, not one superfluous phrase. It is direct, concise, and perfectly complete. It tells us what occurred in the very *beginning* of time, and no editor would dare to alter a syllable of it.

The remaining forty-nine chapters tell us principally about a group of people, beginning with Adam and ending with Joseph, with very specific accounts of their personal lives, their successes, and their failures. Of course there is much more that it tells us, but it is essentially about these men and their relationship with God.

There are few Bible scholars who dispute that Moses wrote the Book of Genesis, although there is no mention in Genesis of the actual author, nor any reference to Moses receiving a revelation from God about what the book contains. It has been a puzzle to Bible scholars through the ages just how Moses could have possibly known these events, people, places, and exact circumstances and incidents contained in this book. He was certainly not present when they took place, for he was born several hundred years after the death of Joseph — the last event recorded in Genesis. But Moses writes with authority and absolute certainty concerning these things.

How did Moses know?

I believe that the answer has been found!

It is astonishingly simple!

Moses was not the author of Genesis, but the *editor* of eyewitness accounts.

Moses — the Editor of Genesis

The answer to the question which has puzzled scholars for thousands of years is so astonishingly simple that it is amazing that the solution has not been discovered long ago. Moses *had to have had* in his possession *written* accounts — written by the very people who had witnessed the events, had known the people, had walked in the places, and had observed first hand what is contained in the Book of Genesis — except of course the first time period of the earth's physical formation when there were no men to see directly what was happening.

The solution to this mystery lies within the text of Genesis itself.

I believe that the key to the Genesis enigma has been discovered by the late P.J. Wiseman, and can be found in his book, *Ancient Records and the Structure of Genesis*.[1] Much of this chapter is drawn from this excellent work, with the kind permission of the publisher.

Air Commodore P.J. Wiseman was a British Royal Air Force officer stationed for a considerable time in Iraq where he became interested in ancient Babylonian clay tablets unearthed in archaeological excavations. Commodore Wiseman was particularly struck by the similarity of how these ancient tablets were structured in relation to the sequences evident in the Book of Genesis. They both, he found, used a repetition of certain words to mark where one account ended and another began. These words comprised what is called a colophon.

The Babylonian tablets often contained subject matter which was too long to be included on only one tablet. In order for a reader to find the continuing tablet, the last few words of the first tablet was written at the beginning of the next one. If a third or fourth tablet were necessary, each would start with the last words of the preceding clay tablet.

The Colophones in Genesis

Commodore Wiseman discovered that in the Book of Genesis the words "These are the generations of . . ." occurred eleven times, and at precisely where they would have been expected to appear if the material they contained had been transcribed from a typical clay tablet found in the excavation of ancient sites in Babylon. Could it be possible that Moses had such ancient clay tablets in his possession when he wrote Genesis?

Commodore Wiseman's interest was aroused and he continued his research into this possibility. First, if this were true, then the art of writing itself must date back to beyond the time of Noah's flood, for Wiseman suspected that the inclusion of the colophon indicated that each segment of the Book of Genesis had been written by a person living at the very time the events described in Genesis had occurred. He began to investigate just how far back in history writing had begun.

How Far Back Did Writing Exist?

From recent archaeological finds it is evident that highly advanced civilizations existed in Mesopotamia very early in history. Not only are the usual artifacts such as pottery found, but clay tablets and stone monuments inscribed with writing have been unearthed. It is clear that the art of writing came in a very early period of time. But how early?

Wiseman found that not only have archaeologists found written records dating to a time immediately after the time of the biblical Flood, but there are in existence several tablets which must have been inscribed before that great Flood.

Sir Leonard Wooley has found at Ur several seals belonging to men who lived before the earth was inundated with water and, as the Bible tells us, all life was lost except that on the ark with Noah's family. From this it is evident that writing was actually in use in the time period covered by some of the earliest narratives found in Genesis.

There is little doubt that the first writers used a wedge to make marks in soft clay. When the clay hardened, and especially if it was fired, the tablet of clay became as hard as stone — and almost as durable. This type of cuneiform writing was used extensively throughout the entire area. Clay tablets containing letters and lists of stores have been found over a wide geographic range, indicating that it could have been understood by people among the nations of the then known civilized world of that time. For this to be true there must have been a common language, at least of communication and commerce.

Did Adam Write the Story of Creation?

Tracing back the genealogical records of the patriarchs as they are listed in Genesis, we come to the conclusion that Adam would have lived in about 4000 B.C. This is neither the time nor place to discuss the findings of paleontologists concerning homo sapiens remains much earlier than that. The Bible tells us that Adam was the first *living soul* and that, I believe, is quite different from what paleontologists have unearthed. For a discussion of this, if you are interested, please see my previous book, *A Scientific Approach to Christianity*, where I give a detailed explanation.

Of course there could not have been any eyewitnesses to relate what we are told in Genesis 1:1 through Genesis 2:7, for Adam had not yet been created. This narrative, however, does suggest a personal account, told by someone who *knew* what had happened. Wiseman believes that this account was written by Adam based on what God had told him. There, in simple language which Adam could have understood, is God's explanation to Adam of His creation of the earth and the creatures which inhabited it, *before* He had created Adam.

In this portion of Genesis is repeated over and over the statements "And God said . . ." and "God called . . .", which certainly indicate that the writer had firsthand knowledge of what had happened during the creation period. This would only have been possible if God himself had *told* Adam what He had done and what He had said. Wiseman points out that in this text the sun and moon are not yet given names, simply being called the greater and lesser lights. This is an extremely important clue, as we will soon see.

If, as some biblical scholars claim, the creation story had been handed down orally for a long period of time, and some suggest as long as until the time of the Exodus, then the sun and moon would have been called by the names assigned to them later. Very early in history both the sun and moon were worshipped, and very early in history they were given names by various cultures. Some of the most ancient Babylonian temples discovered were dedicated to either *sammas,* the sun god, or to *sin,* the moon goddess. Yet in Genesis we find no names are used for either the sun or the moon. The reason for this must be that this account of creation was written before any names had been given to them.

In Genesis 2:19 we are told that God brought the animals He had created to Adam, for Adam to give them names, and "...whatsoever Adam called every living creature, that was the name thereof." How would later generations know what names Adam had given them? P.J. Wiseman concludes that Adam must have recorded their names. Adam *must* have been able to write!

The First Tablet of Adam

There could have been no human eyewitnesses to the events of the first tablet. It was, I believe, what Adam wrote according to what God told him of the events of creation in language which he and later generations would be able to understand. In fact, these words are very probably exact quotations from God, himself. In a later chapter we will examine Genesis 1:1 and see the evidence which clearly demonstrates that these are indeed the words of God.

The first chapter of Genesis tells us that at one time there was no earth, sun, moon, nor stars. Before creation there was nothing of the physical universe. Then God began His work of creation. It does not explain *how* God accomplished this, only that He did it. And although Genesis 1 is by no means a scientific treatise, what it presents in simple language cannot be contradicted by modern science even today.

The primary reason for Genesis 1 is to state simply and clearly that it was God who created the heavens and the earth. They did not always exist. There was a beginning, and before the beginning of the physical universe, God existed.

The first tablet ends with the first colophon, found in Genesis 2:4, "These are the generations of the heavens and the earth . . . ." Here, the Hebrew word *toledot* is used and is translated as "generations." Wiseman points out that this is not the Hebrew word *dor,* which is used 123 times in the Bible to mean generations. The word toledot should be translated as "history," and most Hebrew scholars agree. The Hebrew tradition concerning the life of Jesus is called *Toledot Jesu*, which is translated as "History of Jesus." Hence, the first tablet, written by Adam, should be called the history of the heavens and of the earth, as related directly by God to Adam.

The Second Tablet by Adam

Beginning with Genesis 2:5 and continuing to Genesis 5:1, we find what must be a firsthand account of what happened next. Here we find the creation of Adam, his wife Eve, and the birth of Cain and Abel. We also read of the first murder, the fall from grace in the Garden of Eden, and all of the events which took place until shortly *before* the death of Adam. Everything contained in this tablet would have been within the direct knowledge of Adam. He quotes certain commandments which he received in direct conversation with God concerning what he may and may not do. He quotes God's statement that Adam needed a helpmate, a wife. Many times we find this quotation prefaced by "And God said . . . ." It is perfectly clear that what we are reading was written by someone who knew exactly what had been said by God. There is absolutely no way that any scribe, writing later in history, could have written this.

The second tablet ends with the colophon, "This is the book of the generations of Adam." Note that it calls itself the *book* of the generations of Adam, signifying that it had been a written document, not an oral tradition passed down by word of mouth.

Genealogies are of great importance in many cultures, and no one holds them in greater esteem than do the people of the Middle East. Even today records are preserved of a family's history and genealogy, passed on from father to son, each generation adding to this written record of that family's historical line of descent as births and deaths occur. It was certainly of no lesser importance in those ancient days, and this is exactly what we find recorded in the Book of Genesis.

Genesis was, and remains for us to read today, the recorded history of the human family; beginning with God's simple explanation to Adam of how He formed the world and created life, and continuing generation by generation of the lineage of that very first human family and their relationship with the creator — God.

The Third Tablet — Noah's Book

This tablet begins with Adam's son, Seth, and ends in the time of Noah before the Flood. Very probably it was Seth who began writing this tablet and it was Noah who completed it.

In this we are told of a return to calling upon the name of the Lord, for Seth had replaced the seed of Abel — whom Cain had killed. Then came a great falling away from the Lord and the wickedness that prevailed upon the earth. Giants are mentioned as the product of the "sons of God and the daughters of men." This will be dealt with in another chapter.

This tablet ends with God's decision to destroy His creation, with only Noah finding favor in His sight. It would be Noah and his family who would be saved from the destruction of the great Flood and would live to repopulate the earth.

In Genesis 6:9 the tablet ends with the colophon, "These are the generations of Noah . . . ." The story concerning Noah would require additional writing, but there was no more space on the third tablet for it. What this third tablet contains is the recorded history from the death of Adam to God's selection of Noah to carry the seed of His creation beyond the Flood. Everything written in this tablet is within the ability of the people mentioned in the tablet itself to have experienced. It is, I believe, their eyewitness accounts.

Noah would have had in his possession not only the tablet he was writing, but also the two previously written tablets. Noah would have possessed the *entire* written history of mankind. He certainly would have carried these precious records with him when he entered the ark to await the catastrophic Flood which God had told him was coming.

The Fourth Tablet — Noah's Sons

This begins with Genesis 6:9b and ends with Genesis 10:1. Noah began the writing of this tablet when God gave him instructions on how to construct the ark. The entire record of the great Flood is contained in it. Theologians have found in the story of the Flood and the salvation of the human race a *type* or *foreshadow* of the redemption of mankind which would be brought about later in history by Jesus Christ.

The waters of the great Flood have been likened to Christian baptism, with the person being submerged in the water of death, then resurrected by the power of Christ's defeat of death by His own glorious resurrection from the grave. The ark itself represents a type of Christ, and mankind can find no safety outside of this ark.

The entire story of the great Flood has been in dispute for many years by scientists and skeptics. They point to similar accounts in Babylonian tablets such as *The Epic of Gilgamesh*. Many have claimed that this portion of Genesis was copied much later from some of these mythological accounts of a flood. Wiseman gives clear and convincing evidence that it was actually the opposite, that the Babylonian mythological stories are really corruptions of the true record given in Genesis and recorded by the man who should know — Noah himself.

This tablet was completed by one of Noah's sons, for in it Noah's death is also recorded. It ends with the colophon, "These are the generations of the sons of Noah . . . ."

The Fifth Tablet — Descendents of Shem

Shem is described as Noah's righteous son. The last tablet, recording the death of Noah, was probably completed by Shem and the entire collection must have passed into Shem's possession and care.

This tablet contains some remarkable information. We are told that all of the earth spoke the *same* language at this time, until the Lord confused their tongues at the time of the destruction of the tower of Babel.

Within these first eleven chapters of Genesis is contained another clue which gives strong evidence that these records were written down in the periods of time in which they actually occurred. These first eleven chapters contain many words of indisputable Babylonian origin, while the last fourteen chapters do not. In fact, the last chapters, which were written after Terah, Abraham's father, left the land of the Chaldees and entered Canaan, contain words which have Canaanite and Egyptian roots. This could not have happened if, as some scholars suggest, this record had been passed down orally and written at a much later date.

The fifth tablet ends with the account of the tower of Babel. The last words of this tablet are the colophon, "These are the generations of Shem . . . ."

The Sixth Tablet — by Terah

The possession of all of the tablets had fallen to Terah, who lived in the city of Ur of the Chaldees. Terah was a descendent of Shem, and this tablet contains his genealogy. This tablet contains only what can be read as the continuity of possession of these tablets: from Shem to Terah — Abraham's father, through the seed of Arphaxad, Salah, Eber, Peleg, Reu, Serug, and Nahor, who was Terah's father.

This relatively short tablet begins with Genesis 11:10 and ends at Genesis 11:27 with the colophon, "Now these are the generations of Terah . . . ."

The Seventh and Eighth Tablets — Abraham's Life

There were so many important events in the life of Abraham that it took two tablets to tell it all. Abraham very probably wrote almost all of these tablets himself, with only his death being recorded by his son, Isaac.

In these tablets we find recorded God's promise to Abraham that his seed would inherit the land of Canaan. The Covenant between God and his descendents would be shown by the circumcision of all males eight days after their birth. The reason why God chose the eighth day will be discussed in another chapter.

Sarah, Abraham's wife, was barren and Abraham had no son. This was a personal tragedy for Abraham, for custom was that the eldest son would inherit the bulk of his father's possessions. Without a son Abraham would have no seed to inherit the promises which God had made to him — including the possession of the land of Canaan.

Abraham had attempted to rectify this by having a son with Hagar, his wife's Egyptian handmaiden, but the Lord had rejected both Hagar and their son Ishmael, and Abraham was forced to send them away. At the time of the Lord's visit to warn Abraham of the imminent destruction of the cities of Sodom and Gomorrah, He had told him that Sarah, long past child-bearing age, would produce the son which would be his heir, and the seed of this child would inherit the promises of God.

In these tablets we also find the prophecy from God that Abraham's descendents would be afflicted in a strange land, Egypt, for four hundred years before they would actually possess the land that God would give them for their own. In the last tablets, and in the records written by Joseph, we find in the Book of Genesis the beginning of the fulfillment of this prophecy.

Indeed Sarah did bear Abraham a son, and in a story of perhaps the strongest faith a man can possibly have, we read how Abraham was willing to sacrifice his only son, Isaac, when God commanded him to do so. At the last moment, of course, Abraham's hand was stayed and the Lord provided a ram for a sacrifice in Isaac's place. But God tested Abraham's faith and he had not been found wanting.

These tablets begin with Genesis 11:27 and continue to Genesis 25:19. Abraham was buried by both Isaac and Ishmael. Included is what seems to be a record kept by Ishmael of his own sons, for we find in Genesis 25:12 a colophon concerning the generations of Ishmael. This addition was probably made by Isaac at the time of Abraham's burial when the two male progeny of Abraham were together to pay their last respects to this great man of biblical history.

The tablets of Abraham end at Genesis 25:19 with the colophon, "And these are the generations of Isaac, Abraham's son . . . ."

The Last Three Tablets — Isaac, Esau, and Jacob

The last tablets which are evident in Genesis tell of the renewal of God's promises with Isaac and about his life; the birth of Esau and Jacob and the events of their lives up to the time when Joseph, Jacob's son, was sold into slavery in Egypt by his brothers. The colophons ending each of these chapters are: Genesis 36:1, "These are the generations of Esau . . . ."; Genesis 36:9, again, "These are the generations of Esau . . . ."; and Genesis 37:2, "These are the generations of Jacob . . . ."

Beginning with Genesis 37:2 we find the story of the life of Joseph and this theme continues throughout the remainder of Genesis. The style also changes, for this portion of Genesis would have been written in Egypt by Joseph and probably on papyrus instead of clay tablets. The last four verses were written by someone other than Joseph, for they tell of his death and that he was embalmed in the Egyptian custom.

In Genesis 50:2-3 we are told that when Jacob died " Joseph commanded his servants the physicians to embalm his father: and the physicians embalmed Israel. And forty days were fulfilled for him; for so are fulfilled the days of those which are embalmed: and the Egyptians mourned for him threescore and ten days." Archaeologists have found records describing the

Egyptian embalming process and it does indeed take forty days. No later writer would have had this type of knowledge of the embalming process then in practice in Egypt.

When Joseph's brothers came down from Canaan to Egypt to escape the famine, we are told in Genesis 43:32 that Joseph did not eat at the same table with them ". . . because the Egyptians might not eat bread with Hebrews, for that is an abomination to them." Wiseman correctly states that this could not have been written at a later date by a Hebrew scribe for that scribe would never have admitted such an affront occurred or have had any knowledge of it.

The story of Joseph's life contains such an intimate knowledge of Egyptian names, places, and customs, that it is quite impossible for any later writer to have known them. It also is full of personal details, events which no one but Joseph himself would have knowledge of. Genesis 37:36 specifically states, "And the Midianites sold him into Egypt unto Potiphar, an officer of Pharaoh's, and captain of the guard." Only someone writing at that time, such as Joseph himself, could possibly have been aware of these specific details.

Genesis 41:45 tells us, "And Pharaoh called Joseph's name Zaphnathpaaneah; and he gave him to wife Asenath the daughter of Potipherah priest of On." The next verse informs us that Joseph was thirty years old when this happened. Again, too many specific details for this account *not* to have been written down *when it happened* by someone who *knew exactly all of these minute details*.

Much the same can be said about all of the previous records. Abraham recorded that when the Lord informed him that Sarah would bear him a son at an advanced age, she laughed as she listened from behind the door of the tent. Who but Abraham would have known something like this? When the servant was sent back to Mesopotamia to the city of Nahor to find a wife for Isaac among his father's brethren, this account, too, is packed with details which only a person intimately involved and living at that time could possibly know.

The genealogies contain not only the names of the sons, but also many include their mother's name and the place of her birth. There is absolutely no way in which all of these details could have been carried from generation to generation by word of mouth. They *had* to have been written down. And Moses, when he compiled the Book of Genesis, had to have had access to these records.

Moses — The Editor of Genesis

There is another clue which establishes Moses as the compiler and editor of the Book of Genesis. The tablets would have contained the *ancient* names of places. In Genesis these names are given, but with the addition of the name *in which they were known in the time of Moses.* Some examples of this are:

Genesis 14:2,8 — "Bela, which is Zoar"

Genesis 14:3 — "the vale of Siddim, which is the salt sea"

Genesis 14:7 — "Enmishpat, which is Kadesh"

Genesis 14:15 — "Hobah, which is on the left hand of Damascus"

Genesis 14:17 — "valley of Shaveh, which is the king's dale"

Genesis 16:14 — "the well Beerlahairoi... between Kadesh and Bered"

Genesis 23:2 — "Kirjatharba, the same is Hebron . . . in Canaan"

Genesis 23:19 — "the field of Machpelah before Mamre, the same is Hebron in the land of Canaan"

Genesis 35:19 — "Ephrath, which is Bethlehem"

When Moses compiled the Book of Genesis, *over four hundred years after Joseph's death,* the names of many cities and towns referred to in the tablets had been changed, or the places themselves had ceased to exist. Sodom and Gomorrah had been completely destroyed. Even though Abraham tells of their cataclysmic downfall, someone writing five hundred or more years after the fact would not have known their exact locations. Moses did because he had the written record of Abraham.

The discovery of P.J. Wiseman of the similarity of the Book of Genesis to ancient clay tablets, with the inclusion of the colophons, is certainly convincing proof that these accounts had been written long before the beginning of the Hebrew captivity in Egypt. The Babylonian words of the first eleven chapters, and the Egyptian root words of the remaining chapters, give compelling evidence of this fact.

These written records, passed from generation to generation, surviving even the great flood of Noah and preserved after Joseph's death in Egypt, had become the only "Bible" the Hebrews had before the Exodus and before Moses wrote the others books of the Pentateuch. They carried God's Word to His people, and especially His sacred promises to them in the Covenant made with Abraham. It was their hope, their dream, and the promise of their future. Without these records they might very likely have ceased to exist as a separate and individual people.

These clay tables, or at least copies of the originals, had to have been available to Moses when he compiled the Book of Genesis, editing only to include the current names of places whose names had changed. No other explanation fits.

Genesis — An Eyewitness Account!

When we open our Bibles now to the Book of Genesis, we should do so in absolute awe. This is not just some concocted story, written by some scribe who attempted to reconstruct events far in the past. *We are reading the very words of eyewitnesses!* We can hear Adam speak, listen to Abraham as he speaks directly with God himself. We can actually *be* with Noah on the ark, and watch with Joseph as the brothers who sold him into slavery are brought before him.

Genesis is *not* fiction but an eyewitness account of actual biblical history. But the greatest gift of this book can be found in the very first chapter. In it, Adam has recorded — for us and all who are willing to hear — *the actual words of God as He describes His creation of the world.*

Can you ever read this book again without the feeling that God himself is speaking, that you are hearing the actual words of Adam, Abraham, Isaac, Jacob, and Joseph? Can you ever again treat this as just another book of the Bible?

And to add to this proof, God allowed another man, thousands of years later, to find a startling mathematical design which begins even in that first book of the Bible and runs all through it. To whet your appetite for this type of proof, in the next chapter we will look at just Genesis 1:1 and see for ourselves an example of this "impossible" mathematical design which our God has placed there for us to see and marvel at.

2

Mathematical Design in the Bible! Impossible — but True!

In the last chapter we examined evidence that the Book of Genesis was actually written from eyewitness accounts of the people who had heard and seen and experienced what this first book of our Bible has to tell us. The first chapter of Genesis is, of course, an exception — for Adam was not present when God created the heavens and the earth and all of the plants, trees, and animals which were created before God created man. Adam's written record which we find in that first chapter is, therefore, what God told him had occurred prior to Adam's creation.

The first chapter of Genesis then, contains the exact words of God which Adam wrote down on a clay tablet. Come on, now! Can you actually expect me to believe that? I can hear the scoffers laughing already!

If you find it hard to believe that what we have in our Bible today are really God's actual words, I hope by the time you have finished reading this chapter your mind will be changed — for the evidence is convincing — and astonishing.

Bible Numerics

Before we look at this mathematical design in Genesis, it is essential that a few facts be explained. The first of these is that before the introduction of the Arabic numbers we use today, the ancient alphabets *were* the number systems. Each letter of these alphabets had a definite and known numerical value, and the letters were used *in place of* numbers. The Old Testament was written in Hebrew, and the Hebrew alphabet is a numerical alphabet.

Each Hebrew letter stood for a certain number and that number is still known today. Ask any Hebrew scholar or rabbi and he can immediately tell you these values. The New Testament was written in Greek, and the letters of the Greek alphabet were also used in place of numbers. These values for the Hebrew and Greek alphabets are illustrated in Exhibit 1.

Hebrew Alphabet		Greek Alphabet	
א	1	α	1
ב	2	β	2
ג	3	γ	3
ד	4	δ	4
ה	5	ε	5
ו	6	ς'	6[2]
ז	7	ζ	7
ח	8	η	8
ט	9	θ	9
י	10	ι	10
כ-ך	20[1]	κ	20
ל	30	λ	30
מ-ם	40[1]	μ	40
נ-ן	50[1]	ν	50
ס	60	ξ	60
ע	70	ο	70
פ-ף	80[1]	π	80
צ-ץ	90[1]	ϙ	90[2]
ק	100	ρ	100
ר	200	σ-ς	200[1]
ש	300	τ	300
ת	400	υ	400
		φ	500
		χ	600
		ψ	700
		ω	800

(1) These letters are the same. The second letter is used when it occurs as the last letter in a word.

(2) These letters existed at the time of the writing of the New Testament but later became extinct.

Now, if the individual letters have known numerical values, we are able to add up the values of letters in words or phrases, or entire verses of the Hebrew or Greek language editions of the Bible, and get the sums of these values.

To illustrate this, let's look at several examples from a Greek New Testament. We will begin with the name *Jesus*.

Jesus = Ιησους

$1 = 10$, $\eta = 8$, $\sigma = 200$, $o = 70$, $v = 400$, $\varsigma = 200$

When we add up the values of the individual letters, we get the number 888. The numerical value then of Jesus' name equals 888.

Let's do this with a few more examples.

Godhead = Θεοτητος

$\Theta = 9$, $\epsilon = 5$, $o = 70$, $\tau = 300$, $\eta = 8$, $\tau = 300$,

$o = 70$, $\varsigma = 200$

The total value equals 962.

Son of Man = υιος του ανθρωπου

$v = 400$, $\iota = 10$, $o = 70$, $\varsigma = 200$, $\tau = 300$, $o = 70$,

$v = 400$, $\alpha = 1$, $v = 50$, $\theta = 9$, $\rho = 100$,

$\omega = 800$, $\pi = 80$, $o = 70$, $v = 400$

The total value equals 2960.

We can do the same with the Hebrew words of the Old Testament. This is a bit awkward for us because in Hebrew we have to read from the right to the left — the reverse of what we are used to doing.

The earth = הארץ

$ה = 5$, $א = 1$, $ר = 200$, $ץ = 90$

The total value equals 296.

Theomatic Numbers

The second fact that must be explained has to do with some

very special numbers called *theomatic numbers*. These are numbers which are capable of being divided into the sum values of words, phrases, or entire verses — with no remainder, or within plus or minus two. We will look at the sums of the Greek and Hebrew words whose sums we have calculated, and divide them by one of these theomatic numbers.

God has chosen the number 37 as His "fingerprint." There are several other theomatic numbers, each one designating something very special, but we will only look at the number 37 for now.

We found that when we added up the values of the Greek letters in "Jesus," the total was 888. When we divide 37 into 888, we get 24. We can also express this as follows:

888 = 37 X 24

The sum of the letters in "Godhead" was 962. When we divide this by 37 we get 26; or we can say that 962 = 37 X 26.

The numerical value of the Greek letters in "Son of man" was 2960. When we divide by 37 we get 80; or we can say that 2960 = 37 X 80.

When we added up the values of the Hebrew letters in "the earth" we found that their sum was 296. Dividing this by 37, we get 8. This can be expressed as 296 = 37 X 8.

To illustrate a few of the countless thousands of times the number 37 appears as God's fingerprint in the Bible, I have listed some of these below. We won't go through each calculation but just give the numerical value of the letters expressed as a multiple of 37.

2 Cor. 4:4 — Christ, who is the image of God = 37 X 105
2 Cor. 4:4 — Image of God = 37 X 37
2 Cor. 4:4 — Christ = 37 X 36
2 Cor. 4:4 — God = 37 X 15
2 Thess. 2:1 — Lord = 37 X 27
Mark 12:29 — The Lord God is one Lord = 37 X 72
Col. 3:24 — The Lord Christ = 37 X 120
Rev. 22:20 — Lord Jesus = 37 X 33
Phil. 2:9 — And gave Him a name which is above every name = 37 X 108
2 Pet. 1:17 — This is My beloved Son = 37 X 111
Luke 20:13 — My beloved Son = 37 X 42

1 John 4:9 — God sent His only begotten Son into the world
   = 37 X 120
1 John 4:9 — His only begotten Son = 37 X 54
Gal. 2:20 — The Son of God = 37 X 66
John 10:36 — I am the Son of God = 37 X 54

As you can see, this theomatic number 37 seems to appear whenever God wants to point out something very special, and this happens throughout the Bible, both in the Hebrew of the Old Testament and the Greek of the New Testament. Could this be a mere coincidence? I'll let you decide. I computed the probability of *only* the eighteen features of 37 we have examined. The probability of just these eighteen multiples of the number 37 appearing by chance is:

   1 in 30,000,000,000,000,000,000,000,000,000.

Ivan Panin — The Father of Bible Numerics

Although many scholars through the ages have been fascinated by the numbers which appear in the Scriptures, it was not until Ivan Panin's exhaustive work on this subject that the full extent of the fantastic numerical design to be found in the Bible could begin to be appreciated.

Ivan Panin was born in Russia in 1885. As a young man he was active in plots against the Czarist government and was arrested and eventually exiled. After continuing his studies in Germany he came to the United States and entered Harvard University. Mr. Panin became a Master of Literary Criticism, writing and lecturing widely.

Ivan Panin was an agnostic, but his work with the classical languages and in textual criticism demanded detailed study of the Greek New Testament. In 1890, as he read a passage in the Greek Gospel of John, he made a discovery which was to launch a lifelong investigation of biblical numerics, ultimately revealing the intricate, unique, and detailed numerical design which runs through the entire Bible.

For fifty-two years, until his death in 1942, Panin labored from twelve to eighteen hours each day, accumulating over 40,000 pages of material on biblical numerics. His published books are still available today.[1] I strongly suggest that if what is presented here has aroused your interest, you will obtain these excellent volumes for continued study of this fascinating subject.

One of the many features which Panin discovered in the Scriptures has to do with the repetition of the number 7. In the last chapter I said that we would examine Genesis 1:1 and see that these were indeed the words of God which Adam had written down. Let us do that now.

The Numerics of Genesis 1:1

Our Bible begins with a simple statement. It is, I believe, a direct quotation written down by Adam of the exact words which God spoke to him as God explained what He had done before He created Adam.

Genesis 1:1 says, "In the beginning God created the heavens and the earth."

You will find the Hebrew words of this text to be exactly the same in any copy of a Hebrew Old Testament. These Hebrew words are printed below and the numerical value of each word appears just below that word. Remember that in Hebrew we read from right to left.

בראשית	ברא	אלהים	את	השמים	ואת	הארץ
In the beginning	created	God	(indef. art.)	the heavens	and	the earth
913	203	86	401	395	407	296

Let us now examine what Dr. Panin found in this one short verse concerning the repeated incidence of the number 7.

1. The number of words in Genesis 1:1 is exactly 7.
2. The total numerical value of the three nouns — God, heaven, and earth — is 777, or 111 X 7.
3. The numerical value of the verb — created — is 203, or 29 X 7.
4. The numerical value of the first, middle, and last Hebrew letters in this verse is 133, or 19 X 7.
5. The numerical value of the first and last letters of the seven words of this verse is 1393, or 199 X 7.
6. The numerical values of the first and last letters of the first and last words is 497, or 71 X 7.
7. The numerical value of the first and last letters of the remaining words is 896, or 128 X 7.
8. The numerical value of the participle, *eth* and the article *the*, each of which appears twice in this verse, is 406, or 58 X 7.
9. The numerical value of the last letters of the first and last

words is 490, or 70 X 7.

10. The total number of Hebrew letters in the seven words of this verse is 28, or 4 X 7.

11. The number of Hebrew letters in "In the beginning God created" is 14, or 2 X 7.

12. The number of Hebrew letters in "the heavens and the earth" is 14, or 2 X 7.

13. The number of letters in the first object, "the heavens," is 7.

14. The number of letters in the second object, "and the earth," is 7.

15. The number of letters in the three leading words — God, heaven, and earth — is 14, or 2 X 7.

16. The number of letters in the four remaining words of this verse is 14, or 2 X 7.

17. The shortest word of this verse is in the middle. The number of letters in this word and the word to its right is exactly 7.

18. The number of letters in the middle word and the word to its left is exactly 7.

In this one verse of only seven words, we find eighteen separate features of the number seven. Calculating the probability of these eighteen instances appearing strictly by chance in Genesis 1:1, we find that the probability is of the order of 1 chance in 10 quintillion.

That's 1 in 10,000,000,000,000,000,000.

God's Fingerprint in Genesis 1:1

In the beginning of this chapter we saw how God has chosen the number 37 as His fingerprint. Could we expect to find this also in the first chapter and first verse of the very first book of the Bible? Indeed, if Adam quoted directly from God himself, we would certainly not be at all surprised to find the Fingerprint of God upon that quotation. Let's find where it is.

1. The numerical value of all the Hebrew letters in Genesis 1:1 is 2701, or 37 X 73.

2. The numerical value of the Hebrew letters in "the earth" is 296, or 37 X 8.

3. The numerical value of the Hebrew letters in "God," "heaven," and "the earth" total 777, or 37 X 21.

In only the seven Hebrew words comprising the very first

verse in the Bible, we have found God's fingerprint *three* times. The probability of this occurring *by chance* in these first seven words is in the order of 1 chance in 50,000.

But we have examined *only* the first verse in the Bible! This mathematical design, with the numbers 7 and 37, along with other theomatic numbers, continues *all through the Bible*. It does not matter whether we look at the Hebrew of the Old Testament or the Greek of the New Testament, this "impossible" mathematical design is to be found.

To make certain that this was not just a natural function of these alphabets, other ancient Hebrew and Greek manuscripts were examined. In these non-biblical writings this design does not appear.

Even with our most powerful computers of today it would be utterly impossible to formulate *one* language whose alphabet could be used to write a single typewritten page containing the type of mathematical design we find in *two* languages and alphabets running through our entire Bible. The significance of this is awesome! This means that God must have overseen the development of the Greek language in which the New Testament was written, and He must have created Adam *already speaking* Hebrew.

There is, in fact, evidence that Hebrew is the root language from which many of the world's tongues have been derived. The fact that letters and international correspondence written on clay tablets in cuneiform could be readily understood by diverse people over a wide geographical area gives strong evidence that there was, indeed, a primary and universally spoken language in ancient times. That would certainly have been the very language spoken not long after the time of Adam.

The fact that the mathematical and numerical designs are to be found in *all* books of the Bible suggests something even more astonishing than God's involvement with the two languages of our Scriptures. Since these books were written by men who lived several thousand years apart, their choice of the exact words and phrases necessary for this design to appear means that God, through His Holy Spirit, must have practically *dictated word for word* what these men wrote.

What we have in our hands today is unquestionably the translation of the true and unaltered Word of God. He has given to this skeptical and sophisticated generation scientific proof of the authenticity of the Bible.

Today, the skeptic has absolutely no excuse!

3

Did Methuselah Really Live That Long? Why Can't We?

The Book of Genesis tells us that the patriarchs who lived before the great Flood of Noah lived tremendously long lives. Methuselah lived longer than any of them, with a lifespan of 969 years. That's almost a thousand years! A man of today lives less than one-tenth as many years.

Did Methuselah *really* live that long?

Were the years *shorter* then?

Why can't people live that long today?

Not only did Methuselah live to an extraordinary age compared to the life expectancy of today, but all of the pre-Flood patriarchs did, with the exception of Enoch, of course. We are told in Genesis 5:24 that God took Enoch to heaven while he was still alive. The average age of these men was 912 when they died. If we believe the Bible to be truly God's Word, then we must accept these exceptionally long lifespans as accurate. But can science offer any explanation for the incredibly long lifespan of those who lived prior to the Flood?

Yes! I believe that science may be able to provide such an explanation, and it has to do with the earth's climate and atmosphere at that time.

The Water Vapor Canopy

The earth had quite a different climate before and after the great Flood of Noah. We are told in Genesis 2:5-6 that ". . . for the Lord God had not caused it to rain upon the earth . . . . But there went up a mist from the earth, and watered the whole face of the ground."

Later, when God decided to destroy life from the earth, we are informed in Genesis 7:4 ". . . I will cause it to rain upon the earth forty days and forty nights . . . ."

It is evident that rain was not a usual occurrence, for there had not been what we call a rainbow before the time of the Flood. Certainly, if Noah had been familiar with rainbows, then the sign which God gave to him — and to all later generations — of the Covenant in which He promised never again to destroy all life by flood would have made no sense. After the Flood rain would fall as a natural and usual method of watering the earth, and rainbows would be seen in the sky.

God explained to Noah in Genesis 9:13-15, "I do set my bow in the cloud, and it shall be for a token of the covenant between me and the earth. And it shall come to pass, when I bring a cloud over the earth, that the bow shall be seen in the cloud: and I will remember my covenant, which is between me and you and every living creature of all flesh; and the waters shall no more become a flood to destroy all flesh."

We see that *before* the Flood it had never rained, but when God commanded the rain to fall, it did. This indicates that there was indeed water in the upper atmosphere, enough water for the rainfall to last for forty days and nights. That's a lot of water!

We are given substantiating information in God's description of creation which leads to the same conclusion. When God explained His creative process to Adam, we are told in Genesis 1:6, "And God said, Let there be a firmament in the midst of the waters, and let it divide the waters from the waters."

The Hebrew word translated here as "firmament" is *raqia,* meaning "sky." This means that God separated the waters *on* the earth from the waters *above* the earth — literally: above the sky, just as clouds appear to be above the sky.

What was above the earth at this time was an invisible canopy of water vapor which effectively shut out the harmful rays of the sun and produced a super "greenhouse effect." The radiation of heat from the earth back into space would have been reduced, and the heat from the filtered sunlight would produce a worldwide stable climate. Our earth was, in effect, a giant, canopy enclosed garden watered by the gentle mists which came out of the ground from the reservoirs of water below the surface. These reservoirs were "the fountains of the deep."

Increased Atmospheric Pressure

Today on earth we live at a pressure of *one* atmosphere at sea level. We feel the weight of all of the air pressing down on the earth equal to a pressure of 14.7 pounds per square inch. We aren't aware of this pressure because our bodies were born into it and it is normal for us. There are fluctuations, of course, because high and low pressure systems are responsible for the weather on earth, but the differences are relatively minor. There are some people, however, who experience a sense of discomfort when the atmospheric pressure changes, and there are those who experience pain in their joints or old fractures as a storm, with the accompanying low pressure, approaches.

If the earth before the Flood had been surrounded by a canopy of water vapor above the troposphere — about ten miles above the earth's surface — it would have *compressed* the air beneath and raised the average atmospheric pressure. Just how much this increase would have been would depend on how much water the canopy contained.

We can only speculate about this quantity of water vapor, but not *all* of the waters which caused the Flood came from rain. Genesis 7:11 tells us, ". . . in the second month, the seventeenth day of the month, the same day were all the fountains of the great deep broken up, and the windows of heaven were opened."

It is evident from this that the waters which were below the surface and had previously watered the earth by the mist, were let loose and contributed to the great volume of water which caused the Flood. It is estimated by Dillow[1] that the equivalent of one atmosphere of water in vapor form rested on top of the earth's blanket of air. This, he calculates, would have been sufficient for a rainfall of one foot of water per day for forty days and nights.

Such a vapor canopy would have produced a far different climate in the time before the Flood, and possibly a much different biological system than we have today. The pressure at sea level would have been *two* atmospheres, or about thirty pounds per square inch — twice that of today.

This increased pressure could have resulted in a greater oxidation rate, a much more efficient metabolism, and stronger and more healthy people. The shielding of the vapor canopy would have eliminated almost all genetic mutation from harmful solar radiation. Many pathogenic bacteria may not have existed at all in this environment. We use the term "hot house plant" to designate those grown under ideal conditions, sheltered from storms, furnished with more than ample nutrients, well watered, and ideally cared for. With the benefits provided by the environment under the canopy of water vapor before the Flood, the patriarchs could have been examples of "hot house humans," living under ideal circumstances for a long and healthy life.

Dr. Larry Vardiman[2] gives some additional examples of the benefits of living under increased atmospheric pressure. He states that during the Aquanaut program it was discovered that a cut on one aquanaut's hand healed completely in twenty-four hours while submerged in a diving bell. Based on this observation, experiments in hyperbaric surgery were performed with excellent results. Higher atmospheric pressure has also been found to bring relief from some effects of aging and to help cure certain diseases.

Evidence of a Prior Higher Atmospheric Pressure

With the water vapor canopy no longer in existence, it is impossible to find direct evidence that it actually covered the earth at one time. But there is some very strong indirect evidence that at one time it did exist. This comes in part from the fossils of several prehistoric animals.

Scientists have long been puzzled by the fossilized bones of giant flying reptiles. The pteranodon is one of these, with a wingspan of up to twenty feet. When the weight of this creature is computed and calculations made as to how this large reptile could have launched itself into the air, the problem is quite perplexing. It seems that this animal *could not run!*

How in the world did this huge beast propel itself into the air and take off? Calculations indicate that it would have required a speed of about fifteen miles per hour to become airborne. Could the pteranodon have just flapped his wings and taken off? The calculations say no.

Large birds such as the pelican can take off from a standing position on a pier by facing the wind, spreading his wings, and getting sufficient lift to rise into the air. But calculations tell us that the pteranodon's weight would not allow the animal to do this. But that calculation was based on the present density of the air at today's atmospheric pressure.

When an atmosphere of *twice* that of today is used in this calculation, it is possible for the pteranodon to lift off with only a very light breeze blowing. Airplane pilots know that it is much easier to take off with a heavy load at lower altitudes than it is at higher elevations because the air is heavier. It is clear that when the pteranodon lived the atmospheric pressure must have been higher than it is today — at least twice as high — or this winged animal would have been helplessly grounded, unable to move around, and defenseless against attack. Only the existence of a canopy of water vapor can explain this.

The brontosaurus was a gigantic dinosaur, measuring as much as eighty feet in length and weighing up to twenty tons. It was herbivorous, eating only leaves, shrubs, and the green foliage of the tropical swampland it inhabited. Scientists have long wondered how this diet could have sustained so large a creature, since it would have taken huge volumes of food for it to have grown to this size and to maintain it as an adult.

The vapor canopy, with the resulting increase in atmospheric pressure, would also help to solve this dilemma. Increased pressure would have meant increased oxidation and metabolism. More energy would have come from the food this immense beast consumed so that less food would have been required. Again, the vapor canopy and the increased atmospheric pressure it produced is a logical, and perhaps the only, reasonable answer to this perplexing question.

Since this vapor canopy gave the earth an ideal climate in which to live, people benefited from it as well as plant and animal life. As a result the patriarchs lived to a very old age according to our present day standards. See Exhibit 2 for a comparison of life expectancy before and after the time of the great Flood, as recorded in the Bible. What happened to change all this?

After the Flood the vapor canopy was gone.

The earth's climate was changed.

Atmospheric pressure dropped to what it is today.

Without the protective canopy the earth received more radiation from the sun and genetic mutations occurred.

Man's lifespan was dramatically reduced.

Exhibit 2

AGE AT DEATH

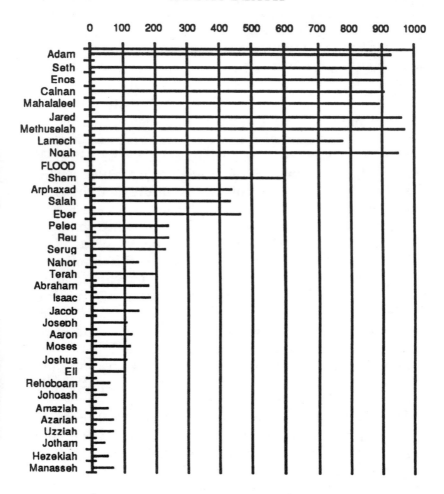

LIFE EXPECTANCY BEFORE AND AFTER THE FLOOD

Did the Great Flood Really Happen?

In the ancient lore and legend of every culture in the world you will find a story of a disastrous great flood. These accounts vary, but in distant parts of the world these stories agree on one point: far back in history there was a cataclysmic flood which wiped out all but a handful of people. From the Indians of North and South America to the islanders of the Pacific, and from the Chinese to at least forty different aboriginal races, we find the elements of a great flood described.

Kang and Nelson[3] illustrate this graphically in the original Chinese characters which are the oldest ideographics in existence. These characters depict elements of the Garden of Eden account and the great Flood of Genesis. These Chinese characters are still in use today to express such extraordinary ideas as *create, naked, righteousness, boat,* and other concepts readily recognizable as biblical in origin.

The fact that almost every culture on the face of the globe has some type of great flood legend with amazingly similar details suggests that these cultures are drawing from a common *past memory* of this event. Since the Bible tells us that it was not until *after* the great Flood that men were scattered over the earth, these cultures would indeed have a shared, but time distorted folk history of what happened at that time.

More Than a Flood — A Cataclysmic Upheaval

Geologists all over the earth find a layer of sediment which gives evidence that there has been a catastrophic worldwide flood. In fact, there are strong indications of much more than just an inundation of water. The cause of this cataclysmic event may well be visible even today, as we will see.

There is general agreement among scientists that at one time all of the current land mass was joined together in one huge continent. They call this super continent Pangaea. Plate tectonics, they say, has allowed the present land masses to break away and gradually drift to their current positions.

Surprising to many scientists, the Bible concurs in several of these points. Genesis 1:9 says, "And God said, Let the waters under the heaven be gathered together into one place, and let the dry land appear: and it was so."

Now, if all the water was gathered together in one place, is it not reasonable to assume that all of the land was also gathered together in one place? Substantiation for this is found in Genesis 10:25, "And unto Eber were born two sons: the name of one was Peleg; for in his days was the earth divided . . . ."

The Bible tells us that immediately after the Flood the earth was divided. Scientists explain the continental drift as a slow process, with the tectonic plates moving at a rate of perhaps inches in centuries. The Bible, however, tells us that during the life of *one man* the earth was divided. This suggests an extremely rapid separation of the land mass, and only a cataclysmic event could be responsible for such accelerated movement of the tectonic plates. Did such an event occur? I believe there is good evidence for just that!

The Hebrew word which is translated "flood" in our Bible actually means much more than what we think of as a flood today. According to Henry M. Morris[4] it implies even more than a catastrophe, nothing less than an earth-changing, world restructuring event.

Is there any scientific evidence to substantiate what the Bible calls "an earth-changing and world restructuring event?" Yes! There is!

When the Earth Split Open!

Dr. Walter T. Brown, Jr.[5] describes the evidence for just such an unprecedented event. The Bible tells us that not all of the water which covered the earth during the Flood came from rain. In Genesis 7:11 we are told ". . . the same day were all the fountains of the great deep broken up, and the windows of heaven were opened." *Fountains of the great deep!* Water *under* the earth!

We know that today the earth's mantle of solid rock, about thirty miles down in depth, rides on the semi-molten and molten rock beneath. Actually the skin on a peach is thicker, percentagewise, than the earth's mantle. We live on a very thin skin of solid material *floating* on the molten interior of this planet.

According to Champ Clark, the earth's total quantity of water is estimated to be 326 million cubic miles. Now, if only *half* of the water of the Flood came from beneath the earth's surface by the "breaking up of the fountains of the great deep," then this would have been a tremendous volume of water. But consider what that would have meant for the thin skin of solid material floating above the molten core of the earth. The single land mass then in existence would have actually been riding on a curtain of steam, since the temperature of the earth's interior is far above the boiling point of water.

There is recent evidence that this was exactly the case, for Soviet drilling engineers have found hot, circulating water at a depth of 7 miles below the earth's surface. This can be explained only by *trapped* water from a pre-Flood earth, for this water cannot possibly be from surface water migrating to such a depth. The weight of overlying rock compress and seal shut even microscopic pores in rock below a depth of 3-1/2 miles. This water must have been part of the original pre-Flood subterranean "fountain of the great deep."

The earth before the Flood was, therefore, a single land mass riding upon a blanket of superheated steam, and with an overhead curtain of water vapor protecting it from harmful solar rays and providing a hothouse climate with an atmospheric pressure perhaps twice that of today. The equilibrium between the earth's crust and the pressure of the superheated steam beneath its surface must have been critical. It would take only a small outside force to upset this equilibrium and rupture the earth's fragile surface, popping it like a balloon.

In God's timing, this is exactly what must have happened. The scar from that rupture may be seen today. It circles the earth in testimony of the cataclysmic effect of what happened in Noah's day when the great Flood occurred.

The Great Scar Surrounding the Earth

In the 1950s Bruce C. Heezen and Marie Tharp discovered a mountain range 40,000 miles long beneath the oceans of the world, which wraps itself completely around the earth. It is called the Mid-Oceanic Ridge. It is composed of a rock called basalt which comes only from deep inside the earth. This is the material of lava flow, and is spewed from erupting volcanoes.

The Mid-Oceanic Ridge is, therefore, the result of a worldwide fissure in the earth's crust which allowed the molten basalt to flow from the core of the earth. This is the scar left from when the earth split open, allowing the superheated steam of the "fountains of the deep" to blast forth into the atmosphere with unimaginable force, providing a major part of the water which covered the earth, and whose sudden rupture not only changed the earth's physical arrangement of land, but the atmospheric pressure as well.

The rearrangement of land is in evidence by examining the continents of Africa and Asia to the east of this ridge and comparing them with North and South America on the west of the ridge. When the coasts of these continents are compared with the Mid-Atlantic Ridge which is part of the overall ridge, we find an almost perfect fit. These four continents were at one time a single landmass, and the rupture of the earth along this ridge has essentially blown them apart.

This redistribution of land on the earth's surface could have happened in a very short space of time, and not the hundreds of millions of years generally attributed to this. With the earth's crust riding on an almost frictionless blanket of steam, the masses of fractured land could have been hurled apart at tremendous speed.

The initial rupture of the earth's crust would have spewed a tremendous jet of superheated steam high above the earth's ionosphere and perhaps beyond. The vapor blanket resting on the air above the earth would have been instantly overwhelmed by the intensity and heat of this supersonic blast and would have collapsed as sheets of worldwide rain. As the rupture of the earth's crust continued, racing quickly around the globe, the release of this superheated steam would have fueled the intensity of the rainfall. The ripping apart of the crust would also have triggered tsunamis of unparalleled magnitude, sweeping the earth with walls of water from the existing oceans.

The split apart landmasses, traveling at great speed on the frictionless water beneath the earth's crust, would have eventually jarred to a halt as the water escaped and the rocks beneath came in contact with the semi-molten magma of the core. But the weight of the land mass, traveling at such a speed, would have suffered the effects of inertia, crumpling the surface and forming great mountain chains. The once relatively smooth and even surface of the earth could have thus thrown up the great chains of mountains such as the Alps, Himalayas, Rockies, Appalachians, Andes, Urals, etc. Look at these great mountain chains and you will find that they are all roughly parallel to the Mid-Oceanic Ridge, which would be expected if this happened.

This would also explain the phenomenon observed in the rocks in these mountains, why they remain unfractured when it is evident that they have been folded over. Any slow force acting on cold rock would have fractured them. Their rapid creation while in a semi-molten state is the only feasible explanation to this.

It also explains the existence of canyons beneath the ocean which are as much as five times deeper than the Grand Canyon with some ten times its length. Some trenches are 15,000 feet below sea level. What gouged them out? It has been proven that the natural ocean currents could not have formed them. In fact, in some of these the currents are flowing in the wrong directions. The only logical explanation is that they were formed by a *sudden* rise and fall of land which could only have occurred during a great cataclysmic event on the earth.

The Instant Ice Age — Quick Frozen Mammoths

The jet of water which gushed high above the earth's atmosphere would have encountered frigid temperatures, converting the water almost instantly to ice crystals. The temperature at 60,000 feet above the earth is about -110° F. These jets of water could have reached altitudes much higher than that, perhaps exceeding 100,000 feet and temperatures less than -200° F.

When the canopy of water vapor which had covered the earth up to that point collapsed in rain, ending the greenhouse effect, the temperatures on earth would have probably been reduced to much the same as they are today. Immediately after the flood, the ice crystals formed high above the earth's stratosphere would have fallen, dumping immense quantities of ice on the earth's polar regions and northern latitudes. This would explain an enigma which has long perplexed science — the discovery of animals which had been quick-frozen in Siberia and Alaska, some still with undigested food in their stomachs and mouths.

Something had happened *instantly* to these animals. No gradually advancing glaciers can account for this, no slowly developing ice age offers an explanation. This happened almost instantaneously, freezing these huge creatures even as they *were chewing their food!*

I don't believe that any other solution to this is possible but that an abrupt and extremely sudden change in temperature, from near tropical to extreme cold, came upon them *within minutes.*

Undersea Mountains Now Cover the Scar in the Earth

When the great fissure broke open in the earth releasing the trapped, superheated steam, the molten magma could then flow. First it tended to fill in the gap left by the water vapor, but as this space was exhausted, it oozed through the crack beneath the ocean floor. The magma would have been cooled as it met the colder water of the seas, forming mountains along the path of the rupture.

These are still evident far below the surface of the Atlantic and Pacific Oceans as the Mid-Oceanic Ridge. This is the world's longest mountain chain, extending completely around the world beneath the oceans. These mountains are the "scab" on the wound which occurred when the superheated steam trapped under the earth's solid crust finally ruptured, changing the earth and its climate in a cataclysmic event which *can never again be repeated on the earth,* for the circumstances which caused it are no longer in existence.

But the evidence of what happened is there. Then, one asks, why hasn't science *told* us about this? Why haven't scientists come to this simple conclusion which explains all of the discrepancies concerning the geological life of the earth? The answer, unfortunately, lies in another scientific delusion — evolution. For in order for the events described here to have taken place, including the great Flood of Noah, they would have to abandon the theory of a slow and gradual change in the geology of the earth — on which evolution is based.

And, of course, they would be forced to admit the existence of God.

Did Methuselah Really Live That Long?

Yes, I believe he did! All of the patriarchs, and others who lived before the catastrophic events which caused the Flood, lived lifespans which today seem unbelievable. The reason for this is that they lived in a world totally different than the world of today.

In fact, when God decided to destroy life upon the face of the earth and begin it anew with Noah's family, He pronounced the sentence of this drastically *reduced* lifespan for men. Genesis 6:3 says, "And the Lord said, My spirit shall not always strive with man, for that he also is flesh: yet his days shall be an hundred and twenty years."

Here we see that God, who had allowed man to live for close to a thousand years before the Flood, declares a life expectancy of a hundred and twenty years for man *after* the Flood. That this is what happened is demonstrated graphically by the chart labeled Exhibit 1.

Why Can't We Live That Long Today?

There are many reasons, one of which is that God said we

couldn't. He changed the environment of the world. The protective canopy of water vapor was removed when the Flood destroyed life on the earth. Now the harmful radiation from the sun could damage the earth's creatures, causing mutations in the genetic process. Bacteria which was passive toward man and animals became, through mutations, pathogenic. Disease came upon the earth.

The atmospheric pressure was reduced by about half. No longer would man and animals receive the benefits of greater metabolic function. More food and nutrients would be required to sustain life. Accidental wounds which had previously healed in hours now took days or even weeks to heal. God changed the rules of the game, and the result was death at an earlier age for both man and beast.

When Adam sinned and was cast out of the Garden, God cursed the ground and created the thorns, thistles, and other weeds which have been the bane of farmers ever since. But the world had remained under the protection of the vapor canopy and its greenhouse environment. Adam may have had to deal with weeds in his fields, but he retained all the other benefits of the perfect climate of the world before the Flood.

We who live in the present time have a natural God-given *biological* clock ticking away within our bodies. God has ordained a pre-set number of years for us to live, and science can do very little to alter it. I know that recent advances in medicine and better nutrition has added years to our lives in the developed countries of the world, but even with this we cannot approach the lifespans lived by those who walked this earth before the great Flood of the Bible.

To end this chapter I want to share another mystery which science so far has been unable to solve — one which illustrates this God-given biological clock within both man and all other living things on this planet. There are several hundred species of bamboo growing throughout the world. Some species survive for decades, some for as many as one hundred and twenty years without flowering — and subsequently dying.

However, when the innate biological clock within *each* species rings, all bamboo plants of that species flower at the *same time* no matter where they are growing in the world. Then, *all* of them die. The seeds produced by the bamboo flowers will produce another generation of bamboo, and this will have the same biological clock ticking away. When this unexplained biological mechanism tells the next generation of bamboo that its life is over, all of them — *worldwide* — will flower and die.

All of them at exactly the same time!

Science can't find the answer to why this happens because science is looking in the wrong place. But those of us who believe that God's Word has all the answers *can* find it, for God plainly tells us. Ecclesiastes 3:1 reveals, "To every thing there is a season, and a time to every purpose under the heaven: A time to be born, and a time to die . . . ." And Ecclesiastes 3:14 tells us why: "I know that, whatsoever God doeth, it shall be for ever: nothing can be put to it, nor anything taken from it: and God doeth it, *that men should fear before him.*"

It is God who is in control of the events of this world. He has been from the beginning and always will be. But those who fear Him have nothing to worry about. He is in complete control, even in the most cataclysmic events imaginable — as we will see in a later chapter.

The Present Lifetime

Later on God further reduced the span of years that was given to man.

Psalm 90:10 tells us: "The days of our years are threescore years and ten; and if by reason of strength they be fourscore years, yet is their strength labour and sorrow; for it is soon cut off, and we fly away."

It is our God, our Creator, who determines the length of our lives. In all probability the mutations which cause disease had come into full sway in the time of David when the Psalms were written. Our biological clock has been set at a much different hour than Methuselah's was before the Flood.

4

Were There Really Giants?
A Scientific Explanation

Genesis 6:4 says, "There were giants in the earth in those days; and also after that, when the sons of God came in unto the daughters of men, and they bare children to them, the same became mighty men which were of old, men of renown."

Were there really giants in the early days of the earth? The Bible plainly states that there were. This passage tells us much more than that, however, for it also tells us *how* these giants came to be on the earth. They were the children of the *sons of God.*

This poses an even more interesting situation, for we must determine something which has been skipped over and avoided by most biblical scholars down through the ages. I might get myself into trouble with some of the conclusions I will draw in this chapter, but be that as it may. We have to try to determine just who these "sons of God" were who produced children, some of them being giants, with the "daughters of men."

First off, the daughters of men had to be people just like you and me. These were women of the human race, descendants of the man and woman by which God populated the earth. That's the easy part. But who are the "sons of God?" I think the Bible tells us that very plainly, too. They are angels!

Job had pride in his own righteousness, and God had to reprimand him. God wanted to know where Job was when He created the earth: "Whereupon are the foundations therefore fastened? or who lade the cornerstone thereof; When the morning stars sang together, and all the *sons of God*

God shouted for joy?" (Job 38:6-7).

Who was with God when the foundations and cornerstone of the earth was laid? Certainly men weren't. But angels were. The shouts of acclaim came from the angels which God had created before the universe, the solar system, and the earth were formed. They are the sons of God referred to in the Book of Job, which mentions them again even more clearly: "Now there was a day when the sons of God came to present themselves before the Lord, and Satan came also among them" (Job 1:6).

Now we all think of Satan as a fallen angel, but I believe that he was much more than that. Later in the chapter I'll explain what I mean by that. But we see in Job that the angels came to present themselves to God, not only in the first chapter, but the second chapter opens with exactly the same statement.

When Satan rebelled against God, one-third of the angels of heaven, the sons of God, also rebelled. We are given a graphic picture of that rebellion in Revelation 12 where Michael and his angels fought against the dragon and his angels. As Satan was cast out of heaven, his tail drew the "third part of the stars in heaven" with him. These were the fallen angels, the sons of God, who had rebelled against their Creator and were cast out with their leader, Satan.

We have tended to think of angels as sexless, but that's really not the case. Just because we are told in Matthew 22:30 that angels do not marry, this does not mean that they could not produce children. In fact, if we men are, as told in Genesis 1:26, made after the likeness of both God and the angels, in their *image*, then it would seem necessary that our entire anatomy is in that image, including our reproductive parts.

Are There Female Angels?

In the Bible where angels are mentioned, there are only references to *male* angels. When the created beings come before the throne of God, they are called the sons of God. Are there any daughters of God? There is no such mention made anywhere in Scripture of female created beings.

But in Genesis 1:26-27 we are told, "And God said, let us make man in our image, after our likeness . . . . So God created man in his own image, in the image of God created he him; male and female created he them."

To whom but the angels could God have been speaking when He said, "in our image?" We see also that He created them male *and* female. But when God created Adam to tend the garden, He made only a man. Adam complained that unlike all of the other creatures which God had created, he had not found a "help-mate" — a creature like himself with which to have a fulfilling, personal relationship. It was only then that God created Eve. I have often wondered why God did not initially form *both* a man and a woman to tend the garden.

If the fallen angels were the sons of God which had been cast out of heaven along with Satan, and there had been no female angels in heaven, it is understandable why these fallen angels then mated with the daughters of man to produce the children of Genesis 6:4, the giants which became "mighty men of renown." Being in rebellion against God, they were no longer obedient to any of God's rules, including sexual abstinence.

The Biblical Race of Giants

These men of renown were fierce warriors and all of the giants mentioned in the Bible are cast in that mold. Goliath is such an example. The Old Testament speaks of giants ten times, including races of men of extraordinary size and ferocity.

When Moses sent the spies into Canaan they brought back a report of giants in the land, the sons of Anak, which made them feel "as small as grasshoppers." David would later face a descendant of these men, Goliath of Gath. In Moab there was also a race of giants called the Emims, and God tells Moses that they are as tall as the Anakims.

In Ammon also had been a race of huge people. The people of Ammon had called them Zamzummins. Joshua encountered Og, the king of Bashan, who was of the remnant of the giants that dwelt in Ashtaroth and Edrei. David fought against another Philistine giant, Ishbibenob, and when the aging David had fainted from the fatigue of battle, Abishai killed the giant.

The Old Testament clearly states that there were indeed races of giants living both before and after the Flood. It also implies that this was the result of the sons of God having children by the daughters of men. From this we can only conclude that the fallen angels were capable of reproduction, and that their children carried the genetic trait of extreme height and extraordinary muscular development.

Gigantism exists today in two types. In one of these, beginning in childhood, overactivity of the anterior pituitary gland results in overproduction of the growth hormone before normal bone growth has been completed. In the other case, hereditary factors which prevent normal ossification at the time of puberty may be absent, allowing continued growth. However, individuals affected by either of these two types of gigantism are muscularly weak. The giants of the Old Testament were fierce warriors, capable of using spears the size of "weaver's beams," and wearing heavy armor and helmets. Their gigantism was not caused by either of these hormonal deficiencies.

Even today there can be men of extreme height who are either muscularly normal or sometimes possessing greater than average strength. The National Football League is a prime example of this. I don't mean to imply that these modern giants are descendants of the union of fallen angels and human women, but it is certainly possible that at least in some cases this could be an explanation. The Bible tells us that there were giants both before and after the Flood. Therefore, the genes which produced these mighty men of renown *must have been carried aboard the ark and survived the Flood.*

Giants in Noah's Ark

Genesis doesn't tell us that Noah or any of his three sons were above average height. For the genetic trait of gigantism to have survived the Flood, then one of the wives of Noah's sons must have carried this gene.

From Chapter 1, "The Genesis Account," we have seen that family records were written down on clay tablets which were then passed on to succeeding generations. The tenth chapter of Genesis gives us a history of Noah's sons and the nations which their children established after the Flood. From this we see that from Ham's son, Canaan, came the tribes which correspond to the areas where the Old Testament tells us that giants lived.

I believe, therefore, that we can deduce that it was Ham's wife who carried the genetic code which led to the races of giants described in the Bible. This was probably a recessive gene, and not all of her children may have carried it, but now and then this genetic code produced men of extraordinary height and strength — the giants.

How Tall Were These Giants?

Height is a relative thing. A young child looks up at his parents and sees them as being giants in relation to his own size. The big bully on the block may be taller for his age than average, but many children don't really start growing in height until their teens. The little boy may become a man of average or above average height.

We know that men of today tend to be taller than their fathers, who were taller than *their* fathers, etc. Better nutrition probably plays a role in the men of today growing taller.

The suits of armor worn by knights of old are impossible for men of today to wear. It appears that at one time men averaged just about *five feet* in height. A man of even average height today would have been very tall in days gone by. What do we know for sure, then, about the height of the men which the Bible calls giants?

We have seen in the last chapter that before the Flood there was a higher atmospheric pressure which probably resulted in a much increased utilization of food. But after the Flood, when the atmospheric pressure was reduced to what it is today, people might have suffered nutritionally and perhaps did not grow as tall. We have seen that their lifespans were drastically reduced — maybe their height was reduced as well.

But just how tall were these giants of the Old Testament? What was the measure of their height? We read in 1 Samuel 17:4 that Goliath's height was "six cubits and a span." What is a cubit? What is a span?

A cubit was usually taken to be the distance from a man's elbow to the tip of his middle finger. A span meant three handbreadths, or the width of a man's four fingers taken three times.

Unger's Bible Handbook[1] lists the span as equal to 8.74 inches, and the cubit, two spans, as 17.49 inches. This would have made Goliath almost nine and a half feet tall. In Deuteronomy 3:11 we are told that the giant Og, king of Bashan, had an iron bed nine cubits — thirteen feet, in length.

But the cubit was the measure from a man's elbow to the tip of his middle finger! Whose forearm was measured? This would have certainly varied from man to man. And if men were smaller in those days, their arms would also have been shorter. In fact, Josephus[2], and some of the manuscripts of the Septuagint, give Goliath's height as four cubits and a span, which would have made him only about six and a half feet tall. Even using the Greek cubit measure he would not have exceeded six feet, ten inches in height.

I don't know what figure is actually correct, but from the Bible we do know that these giants towered over men of normal height, and most soldiers were afraid to engage them in hand to hand combat. David, a young shepherd with a sling — and with God on his side, was not afraid of him. David's courage and faith in the Lord was certainly demonstrated no matter how tall Goliath really was.

Were there really giants in Old Testament times?

Yes, I believe there were.

How tall were they?

We really don't know for certain, but they were much taller than the average man of that day.

5

The Star of Bethlehem!
What Was It?

In the second chapters of both Matthew and Luke we are given the circumstances of the birth of Jesus. Matthew tells us that wise men from the East came seeking this newborn baby and that they had followed a star to find Him. Who were these wise men from the East? How did they know that a child had been born who was King of the Jews, a child whose birth would someday be marked as one of the greatest events in history? What was this spectacular star they had seen and followed? Can science help us to understand these strange events and perhaps tell us what this star really was?

Yes! I believe it can! In fact, much of what we are told in the Bible about the birth of Jesus can at last be explained through what science tells us about some unusual astronomical events which surround the birth of Jesus Christ. We will examine these in detail, but first we have to understand just who these wise men were and what they knew and believed about the bright lights which moved about in the inky blackness of the night sky in that part of the world.

The Magi of Babylon

It is universally accepted that the wise men were Magi, astronomers from what was at one time the Babylonian and Persian empires. It is very probable that these men came from the city of Sippar, which for centuries had been the center of astrology and the science of astronomy which had grown out of it. These were educated men, learned not only in the movement of stars and constellations, but also masters of mathematics. These men not only studied the sky, but were quite capable of calculating the occurrence of eclipses, conjunctions of planets, and the movements of stars.

At the time of the birth of Jesus, astronomy was already four thousand years old. The study of the heavens and the stars was probably one of the first interests of the ancient civilizations, and when you think about it, it is not that surprising. What else was there to do after the sun disappeared over the horizon and darkness fell? There were very few diversions in those days. There was certainly no television, movies, theaters, and the like to entertain people. Books, except for the few who had access to the clay tablets which served as the first books, were not generally available and probably only a few of the upper class could read the cuneiform pressed into the clay by scribes. Only the beauty and mystery of the night sky offered a constant source of wonder, and for those so inclined, an unlimited field of study.

What They Knew About the Stars

No doubt the first discovery made by ancient astronomers was that most of the stars moved about the sky in fixed formations which we call constellations. Some of these formations seemed to circle around a fixed point in the north. These constellations make up what we call the Zodiac. Another discovery, and one which must have provoked quite a bit of speculation, was that there were five stars which moved very rapidly across the sky. It would be learned much later that these were not stars at all, but planets. These "moving stars" would be assigned very special meanings by the ancient astronomers, and some considered them gods moving about in their heaven.

Clay tablets from Sumarian and Babylonian archaeological sites containing astronomical records dating to the second millennium B.C. prove that these early astronomers were surprisingly advanced. They had divided the constellations, which seem to revolve around the north pole, into the twelve signs of the Zodiac which are known today. Their mathematical ability was amazing and they divided the circle of the sky into "houses" for the twelve Zodiac signs, each measuring twelve *ammat,* or 30 degrees. Each ammat was equal to 24 *ubani.*

Our heritage from these early stargazing mathematicians is the division even today of the circle into 360 degrees, a number which reflected the fact that Babylonian mathematics was based on the number 6, while ours is based on 10.

By 500 B.C. they had mastered quadratic equations and had developed astronomical tables which could predict eclipses of the sun and moon, conjunctions of planets, and many other features which modern day astronomers calculate. By the second century before Christ, Babylonian astronomy had reached its zenith and could truly be called a science.

What the Magi Saw in the Sky!

What had the wise men, the Magi, seen in the heavens which led them to come seeking this newborn babe who was to be a king? To answer that, we must remember that almost six hundred years before, the Babylonian king, Nebuchadnezzar, had taken the Hebrews captive back to his kingdom. In 538 B.C. Babylon had been conquered by the Persians and Medes, and Cyrus had allowed the Hebrews to return to their own land.

Not all of the Hebrews chose to return to Judea, however. In fact, less than fifty thousand Hebrews elected to return. The vast majority stayed in the area which had been Babylon and where they had established homes, shops, businesses, raised their children and grandchildren, and felt safe and secure. To go back to a land which most of them had never seen, begin a new life under primitive conditions, and face an entirely unknown future was something they could not consider. So they stayed, and their culture — including what the Hebrews believed concerning certain stars and constellations — stayed with them.

These Magi knew, therefore, that Hebrews considered the constellation of Pisces as representing their own nation. The wandering star called *Udi idim*, which we know as the planet Saturn, designated the city of Jerusalem to the Hebrews. Another wandering star which the Babylonians called *Mul-babbar*, denoted royalty to the Hebrews. We call this the planet Jupiter.

What the Magi saw, then, was clear to them, and it involved the constellation of Pisces, the fish, and the two planets, Saturn and Jupiter. And the Magi knew exactly what these signs in the sky meant to the Hebrews in Judea.

The Signs in the Sky

It began on the evening of May 29 in the year 7 B.C. We can

picture the Babylonian astronomers standing on the flat roof of a mud brick building in the city of Sippar, situated along the Euphrates River about fifty miles north of the city of Babylon. Their eyes were fixed on the constellation of Pisces where a rare event was taking place. The two wandering stars, Mul-babbar and Udi idim, were coming together in the constellation of Pisces. Of course, we know that the planets Jupiter and Saturn were not actually coming together, but when viewed from Earth, their orbits were crossing so that an observer would see them apparently merging together.

This conjunction of Saturn and Jupiter was not in itself amazing, but again on the evening of October 3 of 7 B.C. these two planets seemed to come together in Pisces. When this happened a third time, on December 4 of 7 B.C., we can guess that these men looked at one another in bewilderment. "What could this mean?" they may have asked. Were these strange events announcing something?

They could calculate that once every 804 years there would be a single conjunction of these wandering stars, but three times in a single year! This was indeed a very unusual series of signs in the sky. Their wonder grew as in the spring of 6 B.C. an even rarer event took place. Again in the constellation of Pisces, there was a conjunction, but this time of *three* wandering stars. Jupiter and Saturn were joined by Mars. The astronomers perhaps looked back on this series of events, trying to understand what these signs could mean.

Maybe one of them recalled that Pisces was the constellation denoting the nation of the Hebrews. Another may have added that one of these conjunctions, the event of October 3, 7 B.C., had taken place on what the Jews called their Day of Atonement. Another may have remembered that Udu idim was the star of the city of Jerusalem. They all knew, of course, that Mul-babbar meant royalty. That was it! There was going to be a king born in Judea of the Hebrews! That had to be the meaning, but they would wait for another sign.

That did not come until the following year. They could calculate the conjunctions of the wandering stars. They could predict eclipses of both the sun and moon. But what happened in July of 5 B.C. they could in no way have expected.

Suddenly, in the constellation of Aquila, the eagle, a new star blazed, brighter than any in the sky. In fact, it was so bright that it could be seen even in the daytime. This had to be the sign they had waited for! This brilliant new star must be the announcement of the birth of the King of the Jews!

"I would like to see this child born with such signs in the heavens," one of the Magi might have said.

Another agreed. He would also like to see this great king, one which even the stars of the sky paid homage to.

"Let's go to Jerusalem," a third astronomer may have suggested, and they all agreed. They would journey to Jerusalem of the Hebrews and find this new king that the heavens had declared was being born.

They hurriedly prepared for their long trip. A retinue of servants would accompany them to pitch the tents and cook the meals. They arranged for the camels which they would ride on the journey.

"Presents," one of the Magi declared, "we must take this great king presents." They included in their traveling bags gifts of gold, frankincense, and myrrh. When all was ready they set off for a trip that would be about three months by camel.

"Look," exclaimed one of the men, "the new star goes before us in the direction of Jerusalem. Surely this is a clear indication that we will find this new King of the Jews!"

What these Magi saw is what we today call a nova, an exploding star. It is still there in the constellation of Aquila, the eagle. It is a recurrent nova called Novae Aquila, and it flared up briefly again in 1918, but certainly not as bright as when the Magi saw it. We would not expect it to, for much of the star's gas was expended in 5 B.C. when it announced the birth of Jesus, two thousand years ago. Perhaps it will again burst upon the night sky as a reminder of the glorious event it first proclaimed to the Magi.

The Magi at Herod's Palace

The Magi had left the city of Sippar in July and had traveled along the Euphrates River in a northwesterly direction along the same route that Abraham had followed when the Lord called him out of Ur into a new land. They may indeed have stopped for a few days rest at Haran, where Abraham and his father, Terah, had sojourned until Terah died and Abraham continued on into Canaan.

The Magi then would have traveled southwest, through

Syria and Lebanon until they had reached the land of the Hebrews. We can picture them entering the city of Jerusalem and inquiring where they could find the king's palace. Herod was the king and they would have been directed to Herod's palace.

We can imagine the excitement of Herod's servants when these men and their company of servants arrived. Here were rich men from the East, perhaps even kings, arriving to see King Herod. Herod, being an extremely vain man, would have been flattered that they had come so far to see him. We can picture Herod hurriedly dressing in his finest robes and instructing his servants to usher these strange men into his audience hall.

Herod's enthusiasm would be short lived. "Where," the three Magi asked him, "is the young child that has just been born as King of the Jews?"

Herod was stunned. He was king of the Jews! What was this that these men were telling him? Who was this interloper, this child that they said had been born a new king? Herod would make certain that this child would not live to usurp his own authority!

"Why," Herod surely asked, "have you come so far to seek this child? How do you know that he has been born?"

The Magi would have told Herod about the strange events in the heavens and the sudden appearance of the new and brilliant star that had led them to Jerusalem seeking the child, the newborn King of the Jews. We can sense Herod's anger rising when he heard this story. Herod was not actually a Jew, himself. He had been born an Idumean and had married into the Jewish royal family of Hasmoneans, the descendants of the Maccabees. *Perhaps the priests and scribes know what these men are talking about,* Herod thought to himself. He sent for them to come immediately.

The chief priest recognized what the Magi said. "There is a prophecy," he told Herod, "spoken by the prophet Micah and contained in our Holy books, that a child shall be born in Bethlehem Ephratah who shall be Israel's ruler, the Lord's Chosen One."

Herod scratched his beard and thought. He must find this child and destroy him. He turned to the Magi, and with a false show of piety, he instructed them, "Go to Bethlehem and search diligently for the young child, and when you have found him, bring me word again, that I may come and worship him also."

The Magi left Jerusalem and traveled toward the small town of Bethlehem, just five miles to the south. It was now October and the constellation of Aquila hung low on the southern horizon. The bright nova blazing in that constellation would have appeared to be guiding them as they traveled toward Bethlehem to seek out the child.

The Birth of Jesus

We know from the Gospel of Matthew that they found Him. We are told how Joseph had been betrothed, or engaged, to Mary. We are told about the angel of the Lord appearing both to Mary and Joseph, announcing that she would bear a son begotten by God through the Holy Spirit, although she was a virgin.

Matthew's Gospel tells us that the Magi fell down and worshipped the young child when they had found Him, and that they presented Him with their gifts of gold, frankincense, and myrrh. It is interesting that the Bible really doesn't specifically tell us that there were *three* wise men from the East. We *believe* that there were three because of the three gifts that were presented.

We are further told that the Magi were warned in a dream not to return to Herod, and that after they had seen the baby Jesus, they departed back to their own country by another way.

In Luke's Gospel we are given the story of shepherds being visited by the angel and a multitude of the Heavenly Host, which announced to them that in Bethlehem, the city of David, a saviour had been born which was Christ the Lord. They also went to find the child and found Mary, Joseph, and the baby wrapped in swaddling clothes and lying in a manger. It is important in establishing the birthdate of Jesus that these shepherds were in the fields tending their flocks, for it adds substantiation to the timing of the nova and the visit of the Magi.

In the fields surrounding Bethlehem, shepherds kept their flocks in the fields from May through October. It gets cold during the winter in that part of the world, and sheep are kept within sheltered enclosures during the colder months. The star had first appeared in July, prompting the journey from Sippar of the Magi, a three month trip by camel. It would have been in late October when they arrived in Jerusalem.

I don't believe that the shepherds and Magi arrived at the same time. These two events must have been separated by a period of about a month or slightly more. The shepherds were told "For unto you is born *this day* in the city of David a Saviour, which is Christ the Lord." So it is very evident that the shepherds came to find the baby Jesus on the very night of His birth.

Luke tells us also that *after* this visit of the shepherds, actually eight days later, the infant Jesus was circumcised and the name which the angel had told them should be His name was given to Him. Luke then tells us about Mary's purification according to the Law of Moses.

Under Jewish law, a woman was unclean for forty days after giving birth to a son. For some reason, if she had given birth to a girl, it was a longer period of time, eighty days. Mary, forty days after Jesus' birth, had to offer a sacrifice at a place of worship to complete her ritual cleansing. The type of animal sacrificed depended upon the social status of the family, what they could reasonably afford. A rich woman would be expected to bring a lamb for a burnt offering, while poor women could sacrifice a pair of turtledoves.

Luke tells us that Joseph, Mary, and the infant Jesus went to the temple in Jerusalem to offer a pair of turtledoves for Mary's ritual cleansing. There would have also been a required payment of five shekels to the temple priests for Jesus. This was the "redemption price" given when a firstborn son was one month old, and required by law in Numbers 18:15-16. Joseph, being a devout Jew, would have also conformed with this part of Jewish law.

I believe that the evidence indicates that the Magi found Jesus, Mary, and Joseph soon after this time. Matthew tells us that just after the Magi presented their gifts and had been warned in a dream not to tell Herod where the child was, Joseph also had a dream. The angel of the Lord appeared to him and warned him that Herod would seek to destroy the young child. Joseph was told to take the child and flee into Egypt, until he was told it was safe to return to his own home.

Herod Attempts to Kill Jesus

Herod must have waited impatiently for the Magi to

return. We can picture him pacing the halls of his palace, peering out of the windows, sending his men out to look for the wise men from the East who had come seeking the newborn King of the Jews. Finally, he must have decided they would not return and tell him where the child was to be found.

He knew that the place was Bethlehem. He had inquired diligently of them, according to Matthew, as to just when these strange signs in the heavens had first appeared. They had told him that it had been two years before, in what would have been 7 B.C. according to our calendar, that the first conjunction had taken place in Pisces, the constellation of the Hebrews. *Two years ago!* he would have thought. So the child could be as old as two years by now!

Herod called for his officers to come at once. He could take no chance that this child would live to challenge his own rule. In a terse command he ordered his officers to take their soldiers to Bethlehem. "Kill every male Hebrew child two years of age and under," he ordered.

This would not be such a strange command for Herod's officers, for Herod had not spared even his own sons. During his lifetime Herod married ten wives and had at least fifty children. His paranoia was so great that he ordered the execution of all but a few of his sons, fearing that they would plot to overthrown him and seize power themselves. His blood-lust was known even in Rome, and Augustus Caesar once remarked that it was safer to be Herod's pig than Herod's son, for even though he was not really a Jew he obeyed the Jewish dietary laws forbidding pork. We know of only four of Herod's male children who lived into mature adulthood.

Jeremiah's Prophecy Fulfilled

Herod's officers took their men down to Bethlehem where they killed every male Hebrew child of the age of two years and younger. We can imagine the screams of the mothers as their infant sons were wrenched from their arms and slain before their eyes. Herod had instructed them to go even into the countryside around the town of Bethlehem and kill the children. He wanted no possibility of that one particular child surviving.

Jeremiah had written of that very time, and Matthew tells us of the fulfillment of Jeremiah 31:15. "Thus saith the Lord, A voice was heard in Ramah, lamentation, and bitter weeping; Rachel weeping for her children refused to be comforted for her children, because they were not." Rachel, the wife of Jacob, is the mother-figure of Hebrew women. She died while giving birth to Benjamin and was buried near Bethlehem.

The screams of perhaps hundreds of mothers would have echoed from the hills surrounding Bethlehem that day. But Jesus was safely on the way to Egypt, where he would remain until after the death of Herod. Flavius Josephus, the Jewish historian, in his *Antiquities of the Jews*, tells of the death of Herod, and gives a benchmark which can be verified concerning the exact date. He tells us of an eclipse which dates Herod's death to within a few days of March 13, 4 B.C. If Herod was alive and well when Jesus was born, then Jesus would have had to have been born *before* March 13, 4 B.C. As other events suggest a date in the fall of 5 B.C., then everything fits perfectly with a date of late September to early October of 5 B.C. as the birthdate of Jesus.

Incidentally, Herod's lust for blood extended even to his death. Josephus also tells us that one of the last things Herod did before his death was to order the execution of one of his sons, Antipater. In addition, since he knew that his death would be a cause of celebration and not mourning for the Jewish nation, he ordered that hundreds of the principal men be brought into custody, and when the guards had received word that he was dead, they should kill all of these men. If Herod's death was not to be mourned, then he would cause the entire nation to mourn for those he had slain. This order was not carried out at his death.

Who Saw the Star of Bethlehem?

No records exist in the West or Middle East describing the nova that suddenly appeared in Aquila in July of 5 B.C. How, then, do we know that this really was the Star of Bethlehem?

The first clue came from an excavated garden wall in Rome. This wall, dating back to the time of Augustus Caesar, was painted with a tree. The fruit on this tree were arranged in a very peculiar manner, and it was not until an astronomer saw a picture of this tree that the grouping of the fruit made any sense. He found that the fruit represented stars and they were grouped as the constellations.

But one constellation had an *extra* star. This was Aquila, the eagle, and it contained an extra star. It was determined that the grouping of the constellations were as they would have appeared to someone in July of 5 B.C. in Rome. But what was that extra star?

This mystery was solved when ancient Chinese records were examined. These Chinese records were detailed astronomical observations going back as far as 214 B.C. On a date corresponding to July of 5 B.C., the Chinese astronomer reported a "guest star," a nova, in the constellation which would be Aquila. The records also stated that this guest star was so bright that it was visible even during the daylight hours.

Why was this spectacular star not recorded in the Western world? We really don't know, but there is at least one other occasion where such a brilliant star, or nova, was totally unrecorded in the West, but may be found in detail in the Chinese astronomical records.

In the year of A.D. 1054, a supernova exploded with tremendous energy and brilliance. We can see the remains of it today in what is called the Crab Nebula. The explosion of this star would have been just as bright as the nova in Aquila in 5 B.C., but no Western records speak of it. Again, the Chinese astronomical records do, and they also say that it was so bright that it could be seen in the daytime.

The best explanation as to why these major events cannot be found in Western astronomical records is that astronomy was not considered very important at that time in our culture. The Chinese, however, have always considered astronomy very important. The *Encyclopedia of Ma Tuan Lin* and the *She Ke* contain Chinese astronomical records dating from about 214 B.C. to A.D. 1640.

The Importance of the Bethlehem Star

How important is it for science to give proof and explanation to the biblical account of the birth of Jesus Christ, including Matthew's story of the wise men being led to find Him by the Star of Bethlehem? I believe that in these days of skepticism it is very important.

Consider the significance of the conjunctions of the planets Saturn and Jupiter in the constellation of Pisces, and then the sudden eruption of a nova in Aquila. For these events to have happened, God would have had to program them into the universe at the very moment that the universe was created. Then, at *exactly* the right time, at the very time that His Son was born into the world in Bethlehem of Judea, these stars gave their message to those who understood what the signs in the heavens meant.

God also would have had to lead the Hebrews to choose the constellation of Pisces to represent their nation, Saturn to denote the city of Jerusalem, and Jupiter to mean royalty. He would have had to cause the Babylonian astronomers to acquire the knowledge of what the Hebrew significance of these signs in the heavens meant. We can see the mighty hand of the Creator in all of nature and His handiwork in the heavens.

The Birthdate of Jesus

From the evidence presented here, it is possible to determine within about a month the actual date of the birth of Jesus. Herod the Great was alive when Jesus was born. The Scriptures tell us that he was. Herod died about March 13 in 4 B.C. according to the record of the Jewish historian Josephus, and that date can be confirmed by astronomy, for Josephus tells us it was the night of a lunar eclipse.

The Chinese records tell us that the nova which was the Star of Bethlehem flared into brilliance in July of 5 B.C. The Magi would have arrived in Bethlehem in October, but Jesus had already been born when they arrived. The shepherds were in their fields on the night of His birth, saw the Heavenly Host, and heard the angel's announcement. That night they visited Him in Bethlehem.

Jesus would have been born in the Hebrew month of Tishri. It is very interesting to note that the tenth day of Tishri is the Hebrew Day of Atonement, when sacrifices were made by the high priest for the sins of the people.

Now this is only speculation, but would it not be in God's perfect timing for His Son, who would become the final and ultimate sacrifice for all mankind, to have been born on the Day of Atonement, the tenth of Tishri, in 5 B.C.?

6

When Was the Crucifixion? It Wasn't on a Friday!

Christians celebrate the Friday before Easter as the day on which Jesus was crucified. I grew up believing that this was true, and we called it Good Friday. I never could understand why this day was called "good" when it signified the death of our Lord, but like many others, I didn't pay much attention to this obvious contradiction.

The Friday before Easter really wasn't originally called Good Friday, at all. This misnomer came from the German word *Got*, meaning God, and in German it was *God's Friday*. When German settlers came to this country the word sort of got garbled into Good Friday. But not only is "good" the wrong word, Friday is also wrong. It didn't happen on that day of the week at all.

Passion Week — A Detailed Look at the Days

The climax of Jesus' ministry was the week of His crucifixion and resurrection. This was the prime purpose He had come to earth in human form, to offer himself as the ultimate and final sacrifice for mankind's sins, and in doing so to reconcile sinful man with a Holy God who could not even look upon sin. Let's look at this week in detail and try to determine just when the two greatest events in history actually took place.

The Gospel of John tells us exactly when Jesus came to Jerusalem on that eventful week. "Then Jesus six days before the Passover came to Bethany, where Lazarus was which had been dead, whom he raised from the dead" (John 12:1).

John tells us that Mary and Martha made Jesus a supper.

Mary took a pound of costly spikenard ointment and anointed His feet, wiping them with her hair.

Judas had protested that Mary's ministration had been too expensive, but Jesus remonstrated him. "Let her alone: against the day of my burying hath she kept this" (John 12:7). He knew that only a few days of His earthly life remained.

The supper at Lazarus' home in Bethany was on Friday. The next day was the regular Saturday Sabbath, and Jesus entered Jerusalem riding on a young donkey. We celebrate this day as Palm Sunday, again with the incorrect day of the week.

His entry into Jerusalem was a great event. There had been much speculation whether Jesus would come to Jerusalem for the Passover. The people knew that the Jewish religious leaders wanted to kill Him. When the shout came that He was actually coming, the people cut down branches of palm trees and strewed them on the rocky road leading into the city. Cheering crowds lined the road, hung from the walls around the Eastern Gate, and made the Jewish leaders even more furious with the welcome they gave Him.

All of these events, of course, had been prophesied in the Old Testament. Zechariah 9:9 tells us about His entry on the colt and the triumphant welcome He would be accorded. In fact, almost every event during the week would be a fulfillment of Old Testament prophecy, including the last few hours in which Jesus would fulfill thirty-two individual prophecies. More about these later.

That evening Jesus returned to Bethany with the twelve disciples, and in the morning came back to Jerusalem. This was Sunday, and the temple was full of merchants, selling the birds and animals for sacrifice. "Is it not written," Jesus shouted, "my house shall be called of all nations the house of prayer? But ye have made it a den of thieves."

He overturned the tables of the moneychangers. Since the birds and animals used for sacrifice could only be purchased with temple coins, people had to exchange the Roman currency into temple coins, and with a fee added by the moneychangers. I imagine the priests received a cut of these profits as well.

Jesus left Jerusalem and returned the next morning, on Monday. On the way into the city Peter looked at the fig tree which Jesus had cursed the morning before because it had no fruit. The tree had withered and died. Jesus used this to illustrate His very important teaching of faith and forgiveness found in Mark 11:20-26.

Jesus was confronted by the priests and scribes on this day who questioned His authority. After completely refuting them, He prophesied that the great temple would be destroyed and not a stone left upon another. This was fulfilled in A.D. 70, when the Roman armies, under Titus, demolished it.

On this day He also gave the disciples, and through the Scriptures to us, the signs of the last days before His coming again in power and glory. We can see, perhaps, the priests standing back behind the crowds which surrounded Him as He spoke, their indignation rising as the people paid this itinerant preacher more attention than they did to them. They spoke to one another in whispers, plotting how they might get rid of Him.

Mark 14:1-2 tells us this, and also informs us of the day of the Passover. "After two days was the feast of the Passover, and of unleavened bread: and the chief priests and the scribes sought how they might take him by craft, and put him to death. But they said, Not on the feast day, lest there be an uproar of the people."

This was on Monday. Two days later was Passover, a Wednesday.

This was also the day on which Judas Iscariot sought out the chief priests and made arrangements to betray Jesus. This was the opportunity they had been waiting for, and they could not believe their good fortune. Here was one of that man's own disciples who was willing to deliver Him into their hands. They promised to pay Judas money after he had completed his part of the bargain. Judas made his way back to where Jesus and the others were, and slipped unnoticed among them. They left the city together.

The Day of the Last Supper

On Tuesday morning the disciples asked Jesus, "Where wilt thou that we go and prepare that thou mayest eat the Passover?" (Mark 14:12). This is one of the most misunderstood Scriptures in the New Testament. We must understand how the Passover was prepared, and at what time, in order to see exactly what this verse means. This day was the first day of unleavened bread, the first of seven days in which no leavened bread could be eaten.

We also must understand that the Jewish day began at sunset and continued until the sunset of the following day. Therefore, on this Tuesday the preparations for Wednesday's evening meal, the Passover, would be made. Jesus told two of His disciples, "Go ye into the city, and there shall meet you a man bearing a pitcher of water: follow him. . . . And he shall show you a large upper room furnished and prepared: there make ready for us" (Mark 14:13-15).

How did Jesus expect His disciples to find the *right* man carrying a pitcher of water? After all, the city would be crowded. Could they recognize one man carrying a pitcher? Yes, they could.

The man carrying the pitcher of water would stand out like a sore thumb in the Jerusalem of that day and age. Fetching water was women's work, and very few men would demean themselves by being seen carrying a pitcher of water. The disciples would have no problem at all recognizing this man.

Jesus and the remaining disciples joined the two who had found the man and the house with the large upper room which had been prepared. There they ate the Seder, a meal marking the beginning of the holy days combining the Feast of Unleavened Bread and Passover. It was at this meal that Jesus instituted what we call the communion service, with the bread symbolizing His body and the fruit of the vine symbolizing His shed blood.

In the middle of this meal Judas Iscariot left the room. The disciples thought that since Judas carried the common purse he went to purchase what they would need for the evening meal the next day — the Passover meal. Jesus, of course, knew exactly where he was going. "That thou doest, do quickly," Jesus told him (John 13:27).

After teaching His disciples for the last time, and speaking in words which they should have understood, they left the city and journeyed the short distance across the brook Cedron and up the hill to an olive grove. There Jesus spent His last night on earth in mortal form. We are all familiar with His prayers as He waited for the temple guards, with Judas showing them the way, to come and take Him away. Finally He saw the torches descending from the gate of the city, then climbing up the Mount of Olives toward the garden where He waited.

Judas approached Jesus and kissed Him. This was the sign that the temple soldiers watched for. They quickly seized Him. The disciples started to put up resistance, but soon realized how much they were outnumbered and fled. He was alone. Rough hands pushed Him down the hill, across the brook, and through the city gate. They took Him to the house of the chief priest for the beginning of His trial.

Caiaphas had been appointed as high priest by the Roman governor, Pontius Pilate, to succeed Caiphas' father-in-law, Annas. He had summoned selected members of the Sanhedrin, those who could be counted on to condemn Jesus, for the trial. Nicodemus and others who were known to be sympathetic to Jesus were unaware of this.

We all know the events of that Tuesday night and early Wednesday morning. After the illegal Sanhedrin trial, where Jesus was convicted of blasphemy, He was taken before Pilate. Only the Roman governor could condemn a man to death. Pilate, however, found Jesus innocent. But, politician that he was, Pilate finally succumbed to the pressure of the Jewish religious leaders, and after a staged demonstration demanding that Barabbas be released and Jesus crucified, he allowed the execution to take place.

The Crucifixion — Wednesday

Jesus was scourged and beaten by the bored Roman soldiers who looked upon executions as a diversion from the monotony of garrison duty in Jerusalem. They often forced the condemned to play a game called "The King's Game" in which the prisoner played for his life but had absolutely no chance to win. The markings of this game may still be seen scratched into the original paving stones of Pilate's official residence in Jerusalem.

Jesus was made to carry the heavy cross-bar through the narrow, winding streets to the hill shaped like a skull outside the wall of the city. What a difference a few days had made! Just the Saturday before He had entered the city to a cheering throng. Now, on Wednesday morning, He struggled with the heavy wooden beam, carrying it to His death.

When Jesus arrived at the hill called Golgotha, the Roman soldiers stripped Him. Heavy iron spikes were driven through His wrists into the cross beam. The pain was excruciating as His ulnar and radial nerves were shattered. The cross beam was slipped into a notch in the upright and the "T" shaped assembly was raised. The soldiers guided the bottom of the vertical beam into a hole in the surface of the rock, and the sudden jar sent pain coursing through His wrists. They then crossed His ankles and impaled both insteps with another iron spike driven into the vertical beam.

Crucifixion was death by suffocation, complicated usually by congestive heart failure. The victim had to keep the weight of his body from sagging and compressing the chest. As the victim, usually weakened by the beating received before crucifixion, became exhausted, he was unable to keep the weight of his body from compressing his chest cavity. This not only caused gradual suffocation, but the pericardium began to fill with fluid.

Jesus was crucified at about 9:00 a.m., and died at 3:00 p.m. on Wednesday. Passover, with its traditional meal of roasted lamb, would be celebrated that evening after sunset. At the exact time that Jesus died on the cross the Passover lambs were being slaughtered for the Passover meal.

His body, taken down from the cross without the soldiers breaking His legs as was customary, was buried by Joseph of Arimathaea and Nicodemus in a freshly cut tomb in a garden nearby.

The Jewish religious leaders, fearful that His disciples might steal the body and claim that Jesus was resurrected, requested that a guard be placed on the tomb. A heavy stone sealed the door and a detail of guards began their watch over it.

Jesus was placed in the tomb before sundown on Wednesday. He remained in the tomb during the next three days, Thursday, Friday, and Saturday. In Matthew's Gospel we are told what happened next. "In the end of the sabbath, as it began to dawn toward the first day of the week, came Mary Magdalene and the other Mary to see the sepulchre" (Matt. 28:1).

Why had they waited until Sunday to come? After all, He had laid in the tomb since Wednesday! We all know that the Jewish regular sabbath is observed on Saturday, and that Thursday had been Passover, but what about Friday? Why hadn't they come then?

They couldn't. The day after Passover was an additional

sabbath and the restriction on how far a person could walk on a sabbath was also in effect on Friday. Sunday was the first day in which Jewish women, or anyone else living under Jewish law, could have traveled to the tomb.

Three Days and Nights in the Earth — Why Was This Necessary?

He has risen! After three days and nights in the tomb, Jesus had risen. Why was this time period necessary?

The first reason is that Jesus himself had said He would be three days and nights in the earth. When the scribes and Pharisees asked Him for a sign that He was indeed the Son of God, Jesus answered, "An evil and adulterous generation seeketh after a sign; and there shall no sign be given to it, but the sign of the prophet Jonas; For as Jonas was three days and three nights in the whale's belly; so shall the Son of Man be three days and three nights in the heart of the earth" (Matt. 12:39-40).

There was another good reason for the complete three days. It was the Jewish belief at that time that when a person died his spirit remained within his body for three days. This may have been because it was sometimes difficult to determine whether a person was really dead, or in a coma or a deathlike state from which the person could revive. Even today we read of people spontaneously "coming back to life" after being pronounced dead by a physician. Jews had to be buried by law before sundown, but they received no embalming other than spices being placed around the body and being wrapped in a shroud. Many, perhaps, had revived after having been placed in a tomb cut out of a rocky hillside.

If you have ever wondered why Jesus *consciously* tarried when word was sent to him that Lazarus was dying, this is why. When Jesus finally came to Bethany, Lazarus had been in his grave four days. There could be no questioning by the Jews, after Jesus raised him from the dead, that he had really not been dead at all.

Jesus had to be in the tomb for three days, not only to fulfill His own prophecy concerning himself, but to keep Jews who saw Him resurrected from claiming that He had not really been dead. Everything that Jesus did was for specific reasons, and His timing all had purpose.

What Was the Year of the Crucifixion and Resurrection?

In chapter five we found that Jesus was born in 5 B.C., in the fall of the year. When did the fulfillment of His earthly ministry take place? Can we determine the year of these events as well?

Yes, I believe we can. Luke, writing as a historian as well as an evangelist, gives us some very specific clues we can use. They have to do with the ministry of John, called the Baptist, who was Jesus' cousin, and whose ministry preceded that of Jesus.

In the third chapter of Luke we are told that in the fifteenth year of the reign of Tiberius Caesar, the Word of God came unto John, and that he came into the country around the river Jordan and began to preach. We can, therefore, determine what year was the fifteenth year of Tiberius Caesar's reign, and that would be the year in which John the Baptist's ministry began. Tiberius was the adopted son of Augustus, who died on August 19 in A.D. 14. Tiberius was immediately proclaimed emperor, so that his reign began in August of A.D. 14. But Roman emperors counted the months of the year in which they came to power as their first year, so A.D. 14 was the *first* year of the reign of Tiberius Caesar. The fifteenth year, then, would have been A.D. 28, and John's ministry began in that year.

When Jesus came to the Jordan to be baptized, John was already a famous man in Judea. His ministry had begun the year before and people from all over the area flocked to hear this wild, roughly dressed prophet preach. It was A.D. 29 when Jesus was baptized and His ministry began.

From the events of His life given in the Gospels, we can determine that Jesus' earthly ministry was a period of about three and a half years. We know that the crucifixion and resurrection took place in the spring, for it was at the time of the Passover. If His ministry began in A.D. 29, a year after John's, then the crucifixion took place in A.D. 33.

The year of A.D. 33 as the year of the crucifixion has been substantiated in an article published in the prestigious British magazine *Nature*, written by mathematicians Colin J. Humphries and W.C. Waddington of Oxford University. Based on astronomical calculations and biblical and historical references, these men claim that the only year which fits the evidence with any degree of certainty is A.D. 33.

But is there any other evidence that A.D. 33 was the year of our Lord's death and resurrection? Yes! Let us examine this.

The Sky Was Darkened

Matthew's Gospel tells us that while Jesus was on the cross, the sky was darkened all over the area around Jerusalem: "Now from the sixth hour there was darkness over all the land unto the ninth hour" (Matt. 27:45).

What caused this darkness? Can we find any evidence to substantiate what Matthew tells us? Yes, we can.

Phlegon, a historian of that time, tells us that in Asia Minor, at a place called Nicaea in Bithynia, there occurred a powerful earthquake which raised so much dust, dirt, and debris in a cloud that when it drifted southward it actually darkened the sky over Italy, Greece, and Egypt. Now for this earthquake generated cloud to have reached Egypt from Bithynia, it *had to have* passed over Palestine and would have also darkened the sky over all of that land.

Phlegon tells us that this happened in the fourth year of the 202nd Olympiad, which was the Greek measure of time. This just happens to correspond to the year A.D. 33. We are not given the exact time of the year in which this event occurred, but it is certainly a marvelous "coincidence," which would explain scientifically the darkening of the sky while Jesus hung upon the cross.

Daniel's Prophecy about the Date of the Messiah's Coming

Jesus did not truly become the Messiah until He fulfilled *all* of the Old Testament prophecy concerning himself. Until His resurrection He did not actually conform to every one of them. So it was not until A.D. 33 that Jesus truly became the person spoken of by those who wrote the Old Testament prophecy under the inspiration of the Holy Spirit.

Daniel, during the Babylonian captivity, prophesied the *exact* date of Jesus' becoming the Messiah: "Know therefore and understand, that from the going forth of the commandment to restore and to build Jerusalem unto the Messiah the Prince shall be seven weeks, and threescore and two weeks: the streets shall be built again, and the wall, even in troublous times" (Dan. 9:25).

The weeks which Daniel speaks of are "weeks of years," or seven times the sixty-nine weeks: 483 years. Cyrus, after defeating the Babylonians, had allowed the Jews to return and rebuild the temple which Nebuchadnezzar had destroyed, but he did not allow them to rebuild the walls. Cyrus wanted no fortified city in his realm in which rebellion could develop.

It was not until the time of Artaxerxes in 450 B.C. that Nehemiah was allowed to return and finish building the temple and to rebuild the walls of the city as protection against the Samaritans who tried to destroy them.

When we count the number of years from 450 B.C. to A.D. 33 we get 483 years, exactly when Daniel's prophecy said that the Messiah would appear.

How Long Was Jesus' Earthly Life?

Luke tells us in a rather vague way that Jesus "began to be about thirty years of age" when His ministry began (Luke 3:23). This is the only statement found with which to estimate how old He was. But when we determine the year of His birth, 5 B.C., and His crucifixion and resurrection, A.D. 33, we can see that Jesus was thirty-seven years old when He actually fulfilled all of the prophecy and became truly the Messiah by rising from the dead.

There Is Something Special about the Number 37

In chapter 2 of this book we were able to examine a unique system of numbers which God has chosen to appear in the numerical values of words, phrases, and entire passages in the original Greek and Hebrew texts. The number 37 has a very special place in these numbers, and I call it "God's fingerprint." When Jesus came to earth, He came as "the image of God" (2 Cor. 4:4). When we add up the values of the Greek letters in "image of God," we get 37 times 37.

Let's look at a few even more graphic illustrations of how Jesus is connected with this number. The following is the result of adding up the Greek letters of these words:

Jesus — 37 times 24
Christ — 37 times 40
Jesus Christ — 37 times 64
The Messiah — 37 times 25

There are many more examples, but you can see that there is a relationship between Jesus Christ and the number 37 which cannot be denied. It is not surprising, considering how God has placed these numbers in the Bible, that this is also the number of years Jesus lived His earthly life. Just a coincidence? I don't think so!

Prophecy Fulfilled by Jesus in His Last Twenty-Four Hours

In His last twenty-four hours, Jesus had to fulfill thirty-one prophecies which had been written hundreds of years before in the Old Testament. I am sure that you are familiar with the accounts of that last day when He was seized and taken before Pilate for trial after Judas had betrayed Him, crucified, and buried. Keeping what you know about that day in mind, let's examine these prophecies from the Old Testament and compare them with what actually happened.

1. He would be betrayed by a friend (Ps. 55:12-14; 41:9).
2. He would be sold for thirty pieces of silver (Zech. 11:12).
3. The money would be used to buy a potter's field (Zech. 11:13).
4. His disciples would forsake Him (Zech. 13:7).
5. He would be accused by false witnesses (Ps. 35:11; 109:2).
6. He would be beaten and spat upon (Isa. 50:4-6).
7. He would remain silent before His accusers (Isa. 53:7).
8. He would be wounded and bruised (Isa. 53:5,6,10).
9. He would be nailed to a cross (Ps. 109:25).
10. His hands and feet would be pierced (Ps. 22:16).
11. He would die between two thieves (Isa. 53:12).
12. He would bear shame, reproach, and dishonor (Ps. 69:19).
13. He would pray for His executioners (Isa. 53:12; Ps. 109:4).
14. People would shake their heads at Him (Ps. 109:25; 22:7).
15. He would be ridiculed (Ps. 22:8).
16. People would be astonished (Ps. 22:17; Isa. 52:14).
17. His garments parted and lots cast for them (Ps. 22:18).
18. He would thirst (Ps. 69:3).
19. He would be given gall and vinegar to drink (Ps. 69:21).

20. He would cry out, "My God, my God, Why hast thou forsaken me?" (Ps. 22:1).
21. He would commit His soul to God (Ps. 31:5).
22. He would give a cry of victory and triumph (Ps. 22:31).
23. His friends would stand far off (Ps. 38:11).
24. His bones would not be broken (Ps. 34:20; Exod. 12:46).
25. His side would be pierced (Zech. 12:10).
26. His visage would be marred (Isa. 52:14).
27. His heart would be broken (Ps. 22:14).
28. Darkness would cover the land (Amos 8:9).
29. He would be buried in a rich man's tomb (Isa. 53:9).
30. He would be cut off, but not for himself (Dan. 9:26).
31. He would be the Lamb of God (Isa. 53:7).

Remember, all of these prophecies were in the *Old Testament*, but when we read them it is exactly as though we were reading the Gospel narrative of what actually happened. The odds against one man fulfilling all thirty-one of these prophecies is staggering: 1 chance in 431,696,000.

But Jesus fulfilled another prophecy, the most important of them all, and in doing so truly became the One of whom all the prophecies referred to. God raised Him from the dead (Ps. 16:10).

In His lifetime on earth there were a total of over 300 of them. The odds against one man doing this in one lifetime is: 1 chance in 8×10^{132}. To see just how large that number is, let's put in the zeroes:

1 chance in 8 X 1,000,000,000,000,000,000,000,000,000,000,
000,000,000,000,000,000,000,000,000,000,
000,000,000,000,000,000,000,000,000,000,
000,000,000,000,000,000,000,000,000,000.

Astonishing odds, but Jesus did it. No one except the true Son of God could possibly have fulfilled *all* of these prophecies!

7

Who Goofed with Our Calendar?

We have seen in a previous chapter that Jesus was probably born in what we now call 5 B.C. Since our modern method of dividing eras of time, especially in the western world, consists of time "Before Christ" or B.C., and *Anno Domini*, from the Latin "In the year of the Lord," it is evident that somehow a mistake was made in our present calendar.

What happened to these five years? Who goofed? Can we explain this discrepancy and find out what happened? Yes, we can! But first it is necessary to briefly look at how the various ancient people reckoned a year's worth of time and what they based it on.

Measuring Time

From the dawn of civilization it was found necessary to have some method of measuring the passage of time. It was evident that there were seasons in which crops should be planted, then harvested; religious ceremonies celebrated; and the length of reign of kings be counted. There were two astronomical phenomena on which they could base this measurement: the sun and the moon.

Days lengthened as summer approached, then diminished as the sun became lower in the sky. The concept of the "year" was very much in evidence. But some shorter period of measurement was needed, longer than the day but shorter than the year. The phases of the moon seemed a convenient marking for this period of time.

But things didn't work out right when the moon's phases were used to calculate the whole year. It was observed that the moon's phase period was about 29-1/2 days. Most early calendars, therefore, consisted of twelve lunar months which alternated between 29 and 30 days each. But this didn't quite work out with the solar year.

This method allowed only 354 days, and it soon became clear that the seasons of planting and harvesting were coming earlier and earlier in the year. Something had to be added to the lunar year to remedy this, and many ancient civilizations added an additional month every few years to try to bring things back into conformity with the sun. This didn't work out either, as the solar year is 365 days plus a little less than six hours. All sorts of schemes were devised to correct the lunar calendar, but none were entirely successful.

Among the early people using the lunar year were the Hebrews and the Bible, particularly the Old Testament, reflects this in the observance of the yearly feasts and religious celebrations such as Passover, the Feast of Weeks, Feast of Tabernacles, and other events which mark the Hebrew ritual year.

The Solar Year

At some point in time, certain ancient people discarded the lunar cycles for marking the year and when mathematics had become advanced enough, began to look at the sun for a better measurement of time. The Mayan calendar was based on what must have been very precise solar observations. When the Spaniards conquered these people in the sixteenth century they were amazed at the accuracy of the Mayan calendar.

The Egyptians also had abandoned the lunar year, but they discovered a method of measuring time by means of the helical rising of the star Sirius. They found that 1,461 Egyptian years of 365 days equals 1,460 solar years of 365-1/4 days. This was known as the Sothiacal period, and in 238 B.C. King Ptolemy III decreed the addition of an extra day every 4 years in a manner similar to the leap year we know today. Thus, the solar calendar we use today was begun.

Where Did They Start to Count Up the Years?

Various civilizations counted their years from quite different reference points. In ancient Babylon years were numbered beginning with the birth of King Sargon I, about 2637 B.C. Hebrews began counting years at what would be our year 3761, which they calculate to be the year of creation. Ancient Greeks used the Era of Olympiads, beginning in 776 B.C. Romans used the date of the founding of Rome in numbering their years, and it is this date from which the error of our current calendar has led to the confusion which surrounds the year in which Jesus was born.

The Julian Calendar

In 46 B.C. when Julius Caesar became pontifex maximus of Rome, it was evident that the calendar had become to be out of step with the solar year. On the advice of Sosigenes, an astronomer from Alexandria, he instituted a new calendar which provided an extra day be added every four years to the usual 365 day year. But the men who followed Caesar misunderstood this system and added the extra day *every third year*, throwing the entire Julian calendar off again.

At first this went unnoticed, but as time went by the difference became apparent. In addition, the Christian world did not want the years counted from the establishment of a pagan city, but from the birth of Christ.

The Monk Who Counted Wrong

In the year we now call A.D. 533, the Christian world instituted a new system of numbering years beginning with the birth of Jesus. A monk, Dionysius Exiguus, had made the necessary calculations for this using the old Roman year point of reference from the date of the founding of Rome. But Dionysius used the *wrong* date for Rome's founding. He was off by five years.

How could this supposedly learned monk have made such a mistake? Scholars have debated this for many years, but there seems to be an explanation that fits. With all of the confusion of calendars and the lack of the excellent reference books which we possess today, Dionysius may have arrived at the date he used by counting up the years which each Roman emperor served. Augustus Caesar, however, had first taken office under his given name of Octavian, and had served five years before his name was changed to Augustus. We may never know whether or not this was overlooked by Dionysius and was the actual cause of his miscalculation, but it is a reasonable explanation.

The Gregorian Calendar of Today

The mistake made in adding an extra day every three years instead of every four was finally rectified in A.D. 1583 when Pope Gregory XIII issued a bill containing two chief alterations to the calendar. He dropped ten days from that year to bring things into conformity again with the solar year, and an additional day was to be added at the end of each fourth century to compensate for the small error which still accumulated even with the extra leap year days. This calendar is substantially that which is in use today.

But there is no move underway to correct the mistake Dionysius Exiguus made, and in the year A.D. 1, Jesus was already going on five years of age. I don't think this bothers Him at all. If He were present at creation, which John's Gospel tells us He was, then our calculation of His real age is all wrong anyway. And Dionysius goof gives Bible scholars something else to argue about. Not that they needed it!

8

God's Special Day — the Seventeenth Day of Nisan

In studying the Bible over the course of many years, it struck me that there was one particular day which God seemed to be calling to our attention. On this day many important events occurred, and I decided to make a thorough search through the Bible and record these major incidents. This day is the seventeenth day of the Jewish month of Nisan.

In the last chapter we saw that different people used different methods of measuring time, and their calendars were based on lunar or solar cycles, or a combination of both. The Hebrew calendar is based on the phases of the moon, with the month beginning at the new moon. Each year was actually only 360 days, but to keep this in accord with the seasons, an extra short month was periodically added and the calendar revised on a 19-year cycle.

The Hebrew Day

Our day begins at midnight, but the Hebrew day begins at sundown and ends at sundown the following day. This is very important to keep in mind as we examine this very special day of 17 Nisan which God has made a particular effort to call to our attention in the Bible.

To confound matters, there are *two* Hebrew calendars, a civil and a religious one. As a result, the first month of the civil calendar is actually the seventh month of the religious calendar. If this seems confusing, as I am sure it does, I'll try to make things as clear as possible as we go along.

God Changes the Hebrew Calendar

Until the first Passover, at the time of the Exodus from Egypt, there was only the civil calendar. The year began on the first day of the month of Tishri, which falls in our months of either September or October. Nisan was the seventh month and fell in our months of March or April. But at the time of the first Passover, God revised things and Nisan, sometimes also called Abib, became the first month of the newly established religious calendar which the Hebrews would follow in celebrating the Feast Days and Holy Days: "This month shall be unto you the beginning of months: it shall be the first month of the year to you" (Exod. 12:2).

From that time on the Bible uses this new system of marking the year, although even today the Jewish New Year still begins on the first day of the month of Tishri in accord with the old civil calendar.

God's Special Day

As I began to search through the Scriptures to identify the events which happened on 17 Nisan, I found that no other day, except Passover itself, is mentioned specifically as many times, and the date of Passover is used numerous times in order to pinpoint what actually happened on 17 Nisan. As I found these events all happening on that very day, I became more and more excited. *Why,* I asked, *has God chosen so many extremely important events to occur on that same day?*

Then I realized why. I believe that God's reason is to show us that He is in complete control of the events of this world. He alone ordains the happenings on earth according to His will and, as you will see in many instances, He would have had to place into motion various natural phenomena at the instant of creation for these events to have taken place on that particular day.

The First Event — Noah's Ark Comes Safely to Rest

After Adam and Eve had disobeyed God in the Garden of Eden and had been expelled, their descendants had forgotten God and had become increasingly evil. God decided to destroy His creation, but there was one man who still acknowledged God and was righteous. Noah and his three sons and their wives were chosen to survive. God instructed Noah to build the largest ship ever constructed at that time, and to save a remnant of living things to repopulate the world after the devastating flood.

Noah was ridiculed by others. Here this foolish man was building a huge ship — and probably far from the nearest water capable of floating it — in preparation of a disastrous flood. A flood? How could there be a flood when it had never rained? Noah, obedient to God, continued to construct this ark.

You are familiar with the story of the Flood, so I won't go into detail about it. But one point I do want to mention. When the ark was ready, and Noah had brought the animals into it, we are told that *God closed the door* (Gen. 7:16).

The rain came and the waters rose. I can picture those same people who had ridiculed Noah for so many years now pounding on the door of the ark, pleading to be let in. I believe that even in this the ark represents Jesus Christ, and that many who do not accept Jesus Christ as Lord and Saviour now will have the door shut upon them and that no amount of pleading will let them in after God has closed the door.

It rained for forty days and nights. We are told that the water reached a height which covered the mountains. Many say that this flood never happened, but we have already examined the evidence that it did. Genesis 8:4 says, "And the ark rested in the seventh month, on the seventeenth day of the month, upon the mountains of Ararat."

We must remember that this was according to the civil calendar, and the seventh month was Nisan. Thus, on 17 Nisan the ark came safely to rest on the mountains of Ararat, in what is now Turkey, bringing Noah and his family through the destruction of the rest of the world to start a new life on the earth.

As a scientist I am interested in the statistical probability of all of the events occurring on 17 Nisan. Since there were 360 days in the Hebrew year, the probability of an event happening on any one day is 1 chance in 360. We will keep tabs on the probability as we go along.

The Second Event — Parting the Red Sea

The Hebrew descendants of Jacob had been in Egypt for over 400 years. After Joseph died, there arose a pharaoh who had not known Joseph and the Hebrews had been reduced to slavery. At the time when Moses, the man God had chosen to lead them out of Egypt, had become an adult, they had been given the task of making bricks out of the Nile mud to build the new cities of Pithom (Tell er-Ratabeh) and Ramses (Avaris-Tanis) in the Nile delta. You know the story of how Moses was saved by Pharaoh's daughter and raised as an Egyptian prince, only to give up his exalted position when he killed an Egyptian overseer who was beating a Hebrew. Moses fled into the desert and remained there until God called him into His service at the burning bush.

Moses and Aaron were sent to plead with Pharaoh to allow the Hebrews to leave Egyptian slavery, and the plagues were brought by God to convince him. Only after the first-born of the Egyptians were slain, on the night of the first Passover, did Pharaoh let them leave.

Passover Established

The night on which the first-born of Egypt were killed was the first Passover, for the avenger was to pass over the houses of the Hebrews. They were instructed to kill a lamb and put blood from it on the upper door posts and the two side posts. This was a sign to the Lord's angel to pass by this house and not kill the first born of it, nor the sheep or goats or cattle of the owner of that house. The lamb was then to be roasted for the Passover meal. Exodus 12:14 tells us, "And this day shall be unto you for a memorial; and you shall keep it a feast to the Lord throughout your generations; ye shall keep it a feast by an ordinance forever."

This day was 14 Nisan. It began at sundown. That night the angel of the Lord smote every Egyptian first-born, including the son of Pharaoh. The next morning a great cry went up in Egypt as they realized what had happened. Pharaoh called for Moses and Aaron and told them to take the Hebrews and leave Egypt.

They left the following day, 15 Nisan and we are told the progress of their journey in Numbers 33:1-8. The first night they camped at Succoth. The next day's march took them to Ethan, the next to Migdol on the evening which began the seventeenth day of Nisan.

Pharaoh's heart was again hardened and he sent his chariots after the Hebrews, arriving just as they reached the shores of the Red Sea. Pharaoh thought he had them trapped, but God placed a pillar of fire between the Hebrews and Pharaoh's army. Then, on 17 Nisan, God parted the waters of the sea and the Hebrews escaped across it. When the last Hebrew had reached the far shore God let the Egyptian army follow — to their death — as He allowed the waters to swallow them up completely.

The probability of two events happening on the same day is calculated by multiplying them together — 1/360 times 1/360 = 1/129,000.

Once chance in 129,000 that these two events occurred by accident on the very same day.

The Third Event — The Hebrews Entering Egypt 430 Years Before

This should really be the second event, but the Bible gives it to us after the crossing of the Red Sea. Exodus 12:40-41 says, "Now the sojourning of the children of Israel, who dwelt in Egypt, was four hundred and thirty years. And it came to pass at the end of the four hundred and thirty years, even the selfsame day it came to pass, that all the hosts of the Lord went out from the land of Egypt."

It was not until the Hebrews traveled through the parted waters of the Red Sea that they physically left the land belonging to Egypt, so this was 17 Nisan. This Scripture tells us that exactly to the day, 430 years before, the seventy members of Jacob's family had entered Egypt. This would also have been the seventeenth of Nisan.

Again, we multiply the individual probabilities together to get the calculation of these three separate events happening on exactly the same day — 1/360 X 1/360 X 1/360 = 1/46,656,000. The probability of these three events happening by chance on the same day is 1 in 46,656,000.

Can you begin to see God's hand in the precise timing of things and His control over everything that happens in the world?

The Fourth Event — The Walls of Jericho

After the Hebrews had wandered in the wilderness for forty years, and the generation which had rebelled against God had died, God allowed the tribes to enter into the land which He had promised to the seed of Abraham. Much had happened during these long years. God had fed them with manna and had led them with a pillar of fire by night and a cloud by day. He had given them His laws and the Ten Commandments.

But on several occasions He had come close to destroying them in anger and only the pleading of Moses had changed God's mind. The Tabernacle had been constructed and was carried with them, to be pitched wherever they camped. The ark of the covenant contained the stone tablets of the commandments, a bowl of manna, and Aaron's rod which had budded. The priesthood had been established and leaders among the twelve tribes had arisen. They had started out from Egypt as a rabble; now they were a nation.

Just before entering the Promised Land Moses had died, forbidden by God to enter. Joshua had been selected by God to lead them across the Jordan into their new land. And just as they had left Egypt with the miracle of the Red Sea parting, they entered Canaan by another: God caused the Jordan River, which was in the spring flood stage, to stop flowing and allowed them to cross over on dry land.

They crossed the Jordan and camped at Gilgal (Josh. 5:9-10). They celebrated the Passover at Gilgal, which is only about five miles from Jericho, the walled city which commanded the entrance into the land they were to possess. They would have to eliminate this fortified city to insure their safe passage any farther.

The Conquest of Jericho

Passover is always celebrated on 14 Nisan. Let us follow what the Scriptures tell us happened day by day after that: "And they did eat of the old corn of the land on the morrow after the passover, unleavened cakes, and parched corn in the selfsame day" (Josh. 5:11).

This had been 15 Nisan, and we are told what happened the next day, the sixteenth day of Nisan: "And the manna ceased on the morrow after they had eaten of the old corn of the land; neither had the children of Israel manna any more; but they did eat of the fruit of the land of Canaan that year" (Josh. 5:12).

The corn which the Scriptures speak of is not what we call corn, but any type of cereal or grain. This was probably the ears of wheat, barley, and other grains which had been left in the fields which the inhabitants of Jericho had been harvesting when the Hebrews crossed the Jordan.

We are told what happened next, and with this we must take a step of faith, for although the days seem to be following one another, it is not specifically told to us. But the next passage, Joshua 5:13, tells us that Joshua went to look at the walls of the city, and when he lifted up his eyes and looked he saw a man with a drawn sword in his hand. Joshua went up to this man and asked him, "Art thou for us, or for our adversaries?"

The man replied, "Nay, but as captain of the host of the Lord am I now come."

The angel of the Lord gave Joshua detailed instructions on what the Israelites must do to conquer Jericho, culminating with the walls of the city falling down flat to give them entrance to it. And although it would be seven days before this would be accomplished, on this day, which would have been 17 Nisan, Jericho was given into Joshua's hand.

For many years there has been a dispute among archaeologists about the biblical account of the fall of Jericho. Excavations have revealed that many cities had been built and destroyed on this site, which is probably the oldest city in the world with neolithic settlements dating back as far as 8000 B.C. But the recent publication of an article by a noted archaeologist, Dr. Bryant Wood, has revealed compelling evidence that the Bible is indeed correct in what it says. This, and some interesting scientific data which may indicate what God used to crumble these walls and the means of stopping the flow of water in the Jordan River, will be discussed in a later chapter of this book.

Again, calculating the probability of four events occurring on the same day of the Hebrew year, we multiply $1/360 \times 1/360 \times 1/360 \times 1/360 = 16,796,160,000$. This is one chance in 16 billion, 796 million, 160 thousand.

The Fifth Event — The Cleansing of the Temple by Hezekiah

The next happening which God tells us about in His Word took place about 800 years after the Israelites had entered the Promised Land and conquered it. The time of the Judges had passed, Saul had been made king, then David, then Solomon who had built the beautiful temple for the Lord.

But Solomon, despite all of his wisdom, had taken on the

gods of the foreign wives he had married, and displeased the Lord. When Solomon died the kingdom was divided between his two sons. Then came a period of evil kings and the worship of the Lord in the magnificent temple had ceased.

Israel, the northern kingdom, was the first to feel God's wrath, and He raised up the Assryians to be the agents of His anger. Tiglathpileser led his Assyrian army against Israel and took captive back to Assyria the tribes of the Northern Kingdom. Judah, the Southern Kingdom, was temporarily spared.

In Jerusalem the beautiful temple lay in disrepair. These magnificent buildings, dedicated to God, were now used as garbage dumps, with the porches and halls choked with refuse and waste. Ahaz, the king of Judah, took the silver and gold from the Lord's treasury and sent it to the king of Assyria as a bribe, and the Assyrians did not attack Judah. But the Lord looked upon what Ahaz did as evil, not respecting the treasury of the Lord and not depending upon God for protection against his enemies.

When Ahaz died, his twenty-five-year-old son Hezekiah became king of Judah. This young man worshipped Jehovah and his first concern was to cleanse the great temple in Jerusalem. Let us follow the biblical account of what happened and on what days these events occurred.

In 2 Chronicles 29:1-28 we are told that on the first day of the first month, Nisan, Hezekiah's servants began to cleanse and sanctify the temple. On 16 Nisan they completed the cleansing. Then, on 17 Nisan, the sacrifice and worship again began in the temple.

To calculate the probability of all five of these events taking place on the same day of the Hebrew year, we multiply 1/360 X 1/360 X 1/360 X 1/360 X 1/360 = 6,048,617,600,000. That's one chance in 6 trillion, 48 billion, 617 million, 600 thousand.

The Sixth Event —
Queen Esther Saves Hebrews from Extermination

The next event takes place about two hundred years later. Much has happened in the meantime. After Hezekiah there had been many evil kings of Judah and people had again forgotten their God. The Babylonian Empire had arisen and defeated the Assyrians. Nebuchadnezzar had brought his army to Jerusalem and taken the city, destroying Solomon's temple, and taking the Hebrews back to Babylon into captivity.

Then the Babylonians had fallen to the Medes and Persians. Cyrus had allowed the Hebrews to return home, but many were satisfied to remain in Persia. From the family of one of those who chose to remain came the young woman who would become Queen Esther, wife of King Ahasuerus, better known by his Persian name, Xerxes.

I had often wondered why the Book of Esther had been included in the Bible. It is the only book in which God is not even mentioned. Perhaps it is included because this story relates another extremely important event which occurred on God's special day, the seventeenth of Nisan, and it tells how a courageous Hebrew woman saved her people from extermination at the hand of an anti-Semite named Haman.

One of the Jews who chose to remain in Persia was a man named Mordecai and he was guardian of his brother's daughter, named Hadassah. Mordecai had a mortal enemy, one of King Xerxes' court advisors, a man named Haman. Mordecai had refused to bow down to the presumptuous and vain Haman, and the king's advisor swore that some day he would kill Mordecai.

Xerxes had a beautiful wife named Vashti, and one evening during a drinking party with his cronies, the king began to brag about how beautiful his wife was. Apparently after too much wine, Xerxes decided to show her off to his drunken friends.

King Xerxes sent a servant for his queen to come and dance to show off her beauty. The servant went to Vashti's apartment and gave her the king's order. Now this was in the days when a woman was the personal property of her husband and he could do anything with her he desired. A wife was expected to obey her husband's orders immediately, and to refuse would mean death. This was especially true of a king's order, for the king held the power of life or death over all of his subjects.

But Vashti refused. Xerxes, of course, had been humiliated before his friends. There could be only one punishment, and they all expected Vashti to be executed. The next morning, after Xerxes was sober, he was sorry that he had caused this incident, but the queen must be punished. Not to do so would make the king an object of scorn to his friends — though none would dare do this to his face. Vashti *must* be punished.

But Xerxes loved his wife, and could not bring himself to order her execution. Instead, he divorced her and ordered her banishment. This left the king without a queen, a situation which had to be remedied. His advisors suggested that the fairest of all the virgins of the land be found. After proper instruction and preparation, the king would spend a night with each of the finalists and choose his next queen from among them. The king readily agreed.

Mordecai's niece, Hadassah was very lovely and one of the king's selection committee saw her. She was brought to the palace and included in the group from which Xerxes would select his queen. Of course neither she nor Mordecai mentioned that she was a Hebrew, for there was apparently anti-Semitism in Persia at that time.

After spending a night with each of the chosen maidens, Xerxes chose Hadassah to be his queen. Her name was changed to Esther, a form of the name of the Eastern goddess of love, Ishtar. So a young Jewish girl became the queen of Persia, totally unaware that she would be called upon to risk her life to save her people from destruction at the hand of her uncle's enemy, Haman.

Haman's hatred of Mordecai became an obsession and he devised a plot not only to rid himself of Mordecai, but the land of the despised Hebrews. Apparently he was not aware that the new queen was Mordecai's niece. He tricked the king into signing an edict which would result in the extermination of all Hebrews in the Persian Empire on a certain day that year.

The king's messengers went out from the palace into all the land, posting the king's edict which would command the people to kill the Jews: "Then were the king's scribes called on the thirteenth day of the first month, and there was written according to all that Haman had commanded unto the king's lieutenants, and to the governors that were over every province, and to the rulers of every people of every province according to the writing thereof, and to every people after their language; in the name of King Ahasuerus was it written, and sealed with the king's ring" (Esther 3:12).

What did this edict say?

Esther 3:13 says, "And the letters were sent by posts into all the king's provinces, to destroy, to kill, and to cause to perish, all Jews, both young and old, little children and women, in one day, even upon the thirteenth day of the twelfth month Adar, and to take a spoil of them for a prey."

When Mordecai read the edict posted in the capital city of Shushan, his heart almost stopped beating. All Jews were to be killed and there was only one person who could save their people — his niece, Queen Esther. He arranged to have a message sent to her through one of the eunuch servants of the queen. She sent word back to Mordecai that all of the people should fast and pray that she would be able to change the king's mind. Mordecai spread the word to the Jews of Shushan.

Now let us trace the progress of the events which followed. We were told in Esther 3:12 that the king signed this edict on the thirteenth day of the first month, Nisan. Esther fasted and prayed for three days, and we are told in Esther 5:1 that on the third day, 16 Nisan, the queen put on her royal apparel and stood in the inner court where the king sat on his throne. This was dangerous for her, for to enter this court uninvited could mean death.

Only if the king held out his golden scepter to her would she be allowed to live. Xerxes saw her and her beauty overwhelmed him. He extended the golden scepter and motioned for her to approach the throne. Xerxes asked his queen the nature of her request.

"If it seem good unto the king, let the king and Haman come this day unto a banquet that I have prepared for him," she answered. Xerxes accepted and called for Haman also to attend the queen's banquet.

The feast was a smashing success and the king was well pleased. He probably also drank too much wine. Haman, of course, was both flattered and delighted. Not only had he been able to trick the king into signing an order which would rid him of Mordecai and the rest of the detestable Jews, but the queen had invited him to an exclusive banquet with only the king also in attendance.

Xerxes smiled at his queen and asked, "What is thy petition? And what is thy request? Even to the half of my kingdom, it shall be performed."

Esther answered, "If I have found favor in the sight of the king, and if it please the king to grant my petition, and perform my request, let the king and Haman come to a banquet that I shall prepare for them, and I will do tomorrow as the king hath said."

Xerxes agreed to dine with her again on the next day, 17 Nisan. Haman was ecstatic. The queen had asked him to another banquet the next day. He was certainly coming up in the world. Haman was so elated when he returned home that he couldn't wait to carry out his plan to kill Mordecai. That evening he had a gallows built in anticipation of hanging Mordecai when that day finally came.

But that night Xerxes couldn't sleep. He called for his book of Chronicles and records to be brought and had his chamberlain read to him from it. Written in the records was found an account of a man named Mordecai who had overheard two of the king's ministers plotting to kill Xerxes. Mordecai had reported this and the men had been seized and executed. Mordecai had saved the king's life.

"What honor has been done to Mordecai for this?" the king asked.

The records were searched but nothing could be found. "There has been nothing done for him," replied the king's servant.

The king arose early and went into his court, finding Haman already there, eager to attend the splendid banquet being prepared by the queen. Xerxes asked him, "If the king wanted to honor a man for great service, what should be done for the man?"

Haman of course supposed that the king was referring to him. He thought for a moment, then suggested that the man be clothed in the king's own clothing, be set astride the king's horse, and led through the city where all the citizens would be made to bow to the man.

Haman waited expectantly for the king's answer, but his joy was turned to utter horror when Xerxes told him, "Good idea. Go find Mordecai and you do exactly that to him."

Haman *had* to obey the king's order. So, as much as it galled him to do so, he went to Mordecai, placed the king's royal robes on him, set him astride the king's horse, and led him through the city, calling out for everyone to bow down to him. When this had been done, Haman returned to the palace to attend Queen Esther's banquet.

That afternoon, on 17 Nisan, Esther exposed Haman's plot to kill her people and explained how he had tricked the king into signing the evil edict. Xerxes was furious. He ordered

Haman to be hanged on the very gallows he had built for Mordecai.

The king's edict, stating that all Jews were to be slaughtered on the thirteenth and fourteenth days of the month of Adar, was rescinded. To this day the Jews celebrate those days as the Feast of Purim. During this feast, Jews are encouraged to curse the memory of the man named Haman for what he had tried to do to them. But Queen Esther, a beautiful Jewish maiden, whose name was really Hadassah, meaning myrtle, had saved her people from destruction. That was on the seventeenth day of Nisan.

Calculating the probability of all six of these events taking place on the same day of the Hebrew year, we multiply: 1/360 X 1/360 X 1/360 X 1/360 X 1/360 X 1/360 = 1/2,177,402,436,000,000. That's one chance in 2 quadrillion, 177 trillion, 402 billion, 436 million. We are getting into some astronomical numbers for the probability of all these events happening *by chance* on exactly the same day of the year. Do you think that perhaps God's hand just might be in this?

The Seventh Event — the Resurrection

As we have seen in chapter 6, Jesus was crucified on Wednesday and arose from the dead early on Sunday morning. At sundown on that Wednesday, Passover began. We know that Passover is always celebrated on the fourteenth day of Nissan. Jesus was in the tomb for three complete days and nights in order to fulfill His prophecy concerning the sign of Jonah.

On that first Easter morning, when the most important event in history happened, He arose from the dead on the seventeenth day of the Hebrew month of Nisan.

We calculate the probability of all seven of those events occurring on exactly the same day of the year by multiplying the individual probabilities together: 1/360 X 1/360 X 1/360 X 1/360 X 1/360 X 1/360 X 1/360 = 1/783,864,876,960,000,000. That means the probability of all seven events happening by chance on the same day of the year is an astonishing one chance in 783 quadrillion, 864 trillion, 876 billion, 960 million.

What Does This Mean?

As a scientist, in examining the evidence presented in this

chapter, I can come to only one conclusion: God is very much in control. He is in control not only of what happens in the world, but the exact timing of *when* it happens.

I believe that God has chosen this particular day, 17 Nisan, to show us that He alone determines the course of history. Nowhere in the Bible has there been an effort to pinpoint any other particular day of the year. On no other day have so many important events happened. I believe that this was done so that a skeptical and scientifically minded generation could discover it, and in doing so find indisputable evidence that a higher power not only exists but is in complete control of the events which take place on this obscure planet.

I believe that God has chosen this special day, and the mathematical impossibility of all of these individual events happening by accident or chance on that day, to prove the validity of what is found in the Bible. Consider for a moment that the sixty-six books of the Bible were written over a long period of time by many men. How could there have been any collusion among these men, separated by centuries, in writing these books which point out this one particular day of the year on which these important events took place? It is impossible.

I believe that no intelligent person can come to any other conclusion than that God exists and that He is in control, not only of the past — but of the present and the future.

THE HEBREW CALENDAR

Hebrew Month	Religious Year	Civil Year	Gregorian Months	Special Days
Nisan	1	7	March-April	14 - Passover 21 - First Fruits
Iyyar	2	8	April-May	
Sivan	3	9	May-June	6 - Pentecost
Tammuz	4	10	June-July	
Ab	5	11	July-Aug.	9 - Destruction of Temple
Elul	6	12	Aug.-Sept.	
Tishri	7	1	Sept.-Oct.	1 - New Year 10 - Day of Atonement 15-21 - Feast of Tabernacles
Marchesvan	8	2	Oct.-Nov.	
Kislev	9	3	Nov.-Dec.	25 - Dedication
Tebet	10	4	Dec.-Jan.	
Shebat	11	5	Jan.-Feb.	
Adar	12	6	Feb.-March	13-14 - Purim
Adar Sheni			Inter-Calary Month	

9

Circumcision on the Eighth Day — Why?

The practice of circumcision is a very ancient one, and did not originate with God's command to Abraham as a sign of the covenant. In fact, it was practiced long before by the Egyptians. The word circumcision is derived from the Latin *circumcidere*, which means "to cut around." It is the cutting off of the male prepuce, or foreskin, and has long been widely practiced as a religious rite or a sign that the boy has, in some cultures, achieved manhood. Only the Hebrews demand that this be done on the eighth day of the male child's life, as God commanded it be done.

The Egyptians circumcised boys between the ages of six and fourteen. This ceremony is depicted in a painting at the temple at Karnak, and was practiced at least three thousand years before the time of Christ, and at least a thousand years prior to Abraham's covenant with the Lord. Of the other major world religions, only Islam requires this of its adherents as a sign of spiritual purification.

In other parts of the world, it was practiced among many African tribes, Indians of South America, and among islanders of the Pacific Ocean. It was apparently common among the Edomites, Ammonites, and Moabites of biblical times.

The Babylonians and Persians who ruled over the Israelites for several centuries did not practice circumcision, and it became a special sign of the Hebrew devotion to their God, which puzzled these people and infuriated the Greeks and Romans who later became their masters. In the second century

A.D., the Romans outlawed the practice, but the Jews ignored this and continued. Circumcision was excluded from the Christian requirements after the first Council of Jerusalem, where Paul decried the attempt of Jewish Christians to impose it upon Gentile converts. Among Christian churches, only the Abyssinian Church recognized circumcision as a religious rite to be practiced by its adherents.

Abraham was ninety-nine years old when God spoke to him and made a covenant with him and his descendants. "This is my covenant, which ye shall keep, between me and you and thy seed after thee; Every man child among you shall be circumcised. And ye shall circumcise the flesh of the foreskin; and it shall be a token of the covenant betwixt me and you. And he that is eight days old shall be circumcised among you . . ." (Gen. 17:10,11,12).

So we see that God is the one who ordered the circumcision at a very specific time in the life of a child — at the age of *eight* days. There was to be no variance in this. If the eighth day fell on the Sabbath, or on a Feast Day, it would still be carried out exactly on the eighth day of a male child's life. Why? What was so special about this eighth day? We shall see. God usually has a specific purpose in what He does, and this is no exception.

The Hebrew ritual of circumcision is an elaborate one. The surgery itself is called *brith milah*, and is performed in successive steps. The names of these steps are *mila, periah*, and *metzitzah* in Hebrew. The man who performs the circumcision is the *mohel*. The godfather of the child, the *sandek*, sits in a chair known as *Kisse shel Eliyahu*, or Elijah's chair.

It is at the child's brith milah that he receives his name and the ritual of circumcision brings him under the Abrahamic covenant with God. This ritual and what it signifies has helped Jews through the ages to maintain their sense of nationality and race although scattered throughout many lands and suffering under the persecution of many periods of vicious anti-Semitism.

Why God Specified the Eighth Day

When you cut your finger and it bleeds, a marvelous mechanism within your body is set into motion to stem the flow of blood. It is a highly complex process which takes place in several stages and involves many enzymes and other organic compounds. What happens, and this is a very simplified description, is as follows:

The injured tissue around the wound and the degenerated blood platelets release a substance called thromboplastin.

The thromboplastin converts prothrombin, which is produced in the liver, to thrombin, a clotting enzyme.

This enzyme in turn converts fibrinogen, which is a soluble substance, to insoluble fibrin.

The fibrin forms an organic mesh, the basis for the clot which begins to seal off the wound and stop the flow of blood.

As the fibrin forms, it contracts and squeezes out the blood serum, forming a firm clot.

This is a *very* simplified description of what happens. Many other factors are involved. One of these is the role of vitamin K, which is essential in the human body for the liver to produce prothrombin.

Vitamin K is contained in many foods, including milk. It is the action of the normal bacteria in the intestines which release the vitamin K and allow the body to absorb it for use by the liver in manufacturing prothrombin. But breast-fed babies do not get this essential ingredient for the normal clotting process. Not until the newborn infant is from two to three days old can the bacteria in the infant's intestinal tract begin to release vitamin K in quantities large enough to assure that bleeding from a cut will not be excessive — or fatal in some cases.

It is not until the eighth day of an infant's life that all of the processes necessary to stem the flow of blood reach an *optimum* level. In fact, research has shown that the eighth day is actually the *most favorable* time to circumcise a male infant, for all of the factors required for blood clotting and healing of the wound reach optimum conditions on the eighth day of life.

The Hebrews had no way of knowing this. The fact that blood circulates in the human body was not discovered until A.D. 1616 by William Harvey. But God, who created us, knew *exactly* when the optimum time would be for the carrying out of this sign of His covenant with man. And it was God who told Abraham that on the eighth day the male infants would undergo circumcision, the absolute perfect time in that child's life for it to be performed.

By the eighth day, the infant also had time to recover from the trauma of birth. The infant's natural defense against infection would have had time to gain strength. Within the clot the white cells, the body's line of defense against invading germs, would also have reached an optimum level of efficiency, for in the days of Abraham sterilization of knives was not practiced.

There Is Another Lesson Here

Through the ages, and especially in these days, the Bible has come under increasing attack. Even many Christian denominations no longer believe it to be God's Word. It is, claim Bible detractors, only stories written by men and written down many years after the events occurred, carried by word of mouth, and subject to many errors. The secular world dismisses the Bible entirely, calling it nonsense, fables, tales of folklore accumulated through many centuries by the Jews, and completely irrelevant today.

What these people do not realize, or refuse to recognize, is that the modern science which they so much revere today, is finding that what the Bible says *has basis in scientific fact.* God and God alone in Abraham's time would have known that the eighth day of an infant's life would be the optimum time for circumcision. This was not a lucky guess. It was the pronouncement of the only Person who could have known that the eighth day was the optimum time — the Creator of life himself.

Why would anyone need any more proof than that?

10

The Search for Adam and Eve! Has Genetic Research Found Them?

We all have ancestors. That is an indisputable fact of life. Almost all of us can trace back our family tree for at least several generations. We know who our parents and grandparents were, even our great-grandparents. Those who are interested in genealogy have traced their ancestors even farther back. But none of us can name each and every one of our distant kinfolk back far enough to tell the *entire* story of our family history.

Who were our *very first* ancestors? The Bible tells us their names: Adam and Eve — the first man and first woman according to the Book of Genesis. Evolutionists ridicule this, instead claiming that man is the product of mutational changes — that Homo sapiens are descendants of the higher apes — with the chimpanzee our closest *natural* living relative. They claim that man evolved gradually, and developed from intermediate species in various parts of the world independently.

Those who believe the biblical account of Creation believe that God literally created each species of life as a fully developed life form. That, according to Genesis, included the first man and woman.

It follows that, if the biblical account is correct, we all have this first man and woman — Adam and Eve — as common, primary ancestors.

Who, then, is right about this, and who is wrong?

Can modern science shed any new light on this argument?

Yes! I believe it can!

There are some startling new discoveries in the field of genetic research which may result in paleontologists having to revise their theories on the origin of man.

The DNA contained in the nucleus of each cell of a person was passed on to that individual at the instant of conception — half from the father's sperm and half from the mother's ova. But, in addition to the DNA in the nucleus of each cell, there is a small amount of DNA contained in the mitochondria, the cell's "power plant," located outside of the nucleus. The mitochondria is responsible for providing the cell's energy and is involved in the metabolism and storage of food. This mitochondrial DNA is passed on to succeeding generations *only by the mother*.

This means that the only difference between this type of DNA and that of your ancestors are differences caused by random mutations, and these mutations can be statistically examined all over the face of the globe.

Two biochemists at Berkeley, Vincent Sarich and Allan Wilson,[1] decided to search for clues concerning mankind's origin by examining changes in mitochondrial DNA among the races of man distributed on the major continents of the world. Since the mutation rate over time can be calculated, this should result in information about man's migration from the original *source* of all the mitochondrial DNA. In other words, it should pinpoint just where man began on earth.

In the mid-1980s, Wilson directed this research and it was carried out by Rebecca Cann and Mark Stoneking. These genetic researchers obtained samples of DNA from women living in Europe, Asia, Africa, New Guinea, and Australia, and compared them for mutational differences.

The area which indicated the *most* mutational change would be closest to the source of the *original* DNA, and would indicate where, and perhaps when, man began. The results were amazing.

Paleontologists study fossils. Those whose specialty is early man tell us that we are the evolutionary result of a chain of species of prehistoric hominids including Sivapithecus, Australopithecus afarensis, Australopithecus africanus, Australopithecus robustus, Homo habilis, Homo erectus, and finally modern man, Homo sapiens.

Actually, they tell us that Homo sapiens include Homo

sapiens neanderthalensis, and we are Homo sapiens sapiens — beginning with the Cro-Magnon species appearing about 30,000 years ago.

These scientists study fossilized bones, and from their insistence that they are absolutely correct, one would believe that they have studied *thousands* of bone specimens to reach these conclusions. The fact of the matter is that all of this so-called scientific proof of the origin of man comes from only *a few dozen bones*. If all of these specimens were collected together, they would hardly fill a box the size of a single coffin.

Some of these claims concerning man's early ancestors are based on small fragments of a single skull, bone chips the size of a fingernail, and pieces of what is claimed to be parts of legs, arms, and ribs, with no absolute assurance these parts really came from the same individual. The data is not just incomplete — it is almost non-existent!

Has the Genetic Eve Been Found?

When the results of the mitochondrial DNA research was published in the prestigious scientific magazine *Nature*, it burst upon these paleontologists like a bomb. Their reaction was fast and furious, for it threatened all of their pet theories — and their credibility.

This study presented evidence that the mitochondrial DNA in *all but one* geographic area was extremely similar. Only the DNA taken from groups of African lineage indicated much change in the mitochondrial DNA, indicating that it had been around twice as long as the mitochondrial DNA from the other groups.

In addition, when these researchers calculated the period of time required for this divergence of the African DNA from the other groups, they came up with a date which further distressed the pundits of bones and skulls. The report by Wilson, Stoneking, and Cann contained data indicating that *all* of mankind's mitochondrial DNA originated from *one* woman who lived in the vicinity of sub-Sahara Africa no more than 140,000 to 280,000 thousand years ago. This blew the paleontologists' claims of homid bones millions of years old right out of their laboratory windows.

The authors of this published scientific paper named this woman, whose mitochondrial DNA was the origin of that which is in the cells of every, man, woman, and child living today — *EVE.*

This means that the specimens of bones which are claimed to be from our prehistoric ancestors are not from our ancestors at all. This research shoots down all of the fancy theories of the rise of modern man from such sketchy and shadowy figures as Homo erectus and Homo habilis, and all the rest of the lot with the long, scientific names.

Not only that, but the respected men of science who had advanced these theories were hanging onto a very shaky tree limb. As James Shreeve puts it in an excellent article on this subject published in the August 1990 issue of *Discover* magazine, "Anthropologists themselves, who had spent decades painstakingly tracing the connection between *H. erectus* and modern humans in several corners of the world, were closer than ever to being run off the field of prehistory by the biologists. For example, if the progeny of someone who lived in Java 750,000 years ago were totally replaced by our ancestors who came out of Africa over half a million years later, that doesn't reflect too kindly on the researcher who devoted a career to showing how the Java skull evolved into our own."[2]

The work of Wilson and his colleagues has naturally come under fierce attack by paleo-anthropologists. Evolutionists will never accept it and that is to be expected, for any hint that man is a *recent* creature on this planet takes away the eons of time necessary for the evolutionary theories. The mitochondrial DNA studies need to be expanded and refined, of course, and that work is going on now.

The mutational constant used to determine the maximum time for the African mitochondrial DNA to reach its present form was a very conservative one. I believe that additional work will show that man is an even more recent species than this study indicated. It is possible that after the water vapor canopy fell to earth in the torrential rain of the great Flood, there could have been a sudden and dramatic *increase* in genetic mutations in that part of the DNA most susceptible to mutation by exposure to solar ultraviolet radiation. Indeed, this could bring the estimate of the date of the first female human ancestor within the biblical framework of creation.

The Genetic Search for Adam

Science has apparently found what may be the genetic Eve,

but what about the genetic Adam? Could it be possible that a similar "genetic tag" could be used to locate him?

The answer is YES! And perhaps Adam has also been found.[3] In 1985, geneticist Gerard Lucotte of the College de France in Paris was able to identify a master form of the male Y chromosome.[4] This is known as haplotype XIII, and it is the form of the male Y chromosome from which all other types have mutated. Since the Y chromosome is passed intact from father to son, it should serve as a tracer in the same manner as the mitochondrial DNA used to identify the origin and approximate date of "Eve."

Lucotte analyzed the Y chromosomes of groups of men from various parts of the world in much the same manner in which Wilson and his colleagues sampled the mitochondrial DNA from women. In 1989 he announced his findings. It seems as though this tracer haplotype XIII had originated in Africa, in the same general location as the "genetic Eve" had been located.

But what about the time period? Was this also similar?

Indeed it was! Calculating the mutation rate of the groups of men in much the same way as Wilson and has associates had, Lucotte arrived at a date of approximately 200,000 B.C. for the first genetic man. This was precisely the same time Wilson had calculated for the female counterpart, the primordial "mother" of mankind.

Lucotte's work has come under the same attack as Wilson's from paleo-anthropologists, the "bone, tooth, and skull fragment" people who contend that man's rise from semi-apes was a long and gradual ascent. That, too, was expected, but these two independent and startling research projects in genetics have prompted a flurry of additional research on this subject, and these may well provide indisputable data that the "bone and skull" men cannot refute.

I find it of particular interest that science, which was responsible for the evolutionary theories which led many to scoff at the biblical version of creation, is now leading directly back to the *confirmation* of the biblical time frame of Genesis.

The Significance of These Discoveries

Probably what disturbs the paleo-anthropologists most is that it was not a group of "fundamentalist, Bible believing,

Creation Science" men and women who carried out and published these studies. It was done by respected and fully-qualified geneticists and molecular biologists at prominent research institutions.

It is rather ironic that scientists who themselves probably do not believe the Genesis creation story of the Bible, are supplying the scientific proof of its accuracy. But even unbelievers stumble upon the truth on occasion, even if it is by accident. God has a great sense of humor.

These findings do not mean that Adam and Eve had to have lived in Africa, where the closest match to both the male Y chromosome haplotype XIII and the original female mitochondrial DNA were found. We must remember that Adam and Eve were driven out of the Garden of Eden. Remember, also, that after the earth was destroyed in the great Flood, God commanded that Noah's sons and their wives repopulate the earth. This was not done, according to the Bible, until God confused the language of those who were building the Tower of Babel.

We must also consider that before Noah's time, the Bible tells us that the earth's landmass was a single entity, and it was not until after the Flood, in Peleg's lifetime, that the land was divided.

But these studies do indicate something extremely important for those who believe that the Bible is truly God's Word:

• Science has found a genetic candidate for the biblical Eve.

• Science has found a genetic candidate for the biblical Adam.

• Science has found that these two people lived much more recently than evolutionists claim.

• The theory of evolution has been dealt another stunning blow.

In Genesis 1:27 we are told, "So God created man in his own image, in the image of God created he him; male and female created he them." God uses the term *created,* not evolved. His Word does not state that He allowed them to mutate from lower forms of life. No mention is made of God producing man from chimpanzees or gorillas. It simply and authoritatively tells us that He *created* them, male and female. In a previous chapter we have seen irrefutable proof that Adam accurately transcribed the very words of God in the first chapter of Genesis.

That's what God said He did, and He did exactly what He said.

Many scientists refuse to believe the Genesis account for one simple reason. They can't, because they do not believe that God himself exists.

But now, by its own hand, science is undermining that disbelief. Perhaps, after all these years of darkness, science is finally catching up with the truth that was right there all along — in Genesis.

11

Just Who Is Satan?

In Genesis 3:1-5 Eve met Satan and this led to mankind's fall into sin. Just who is this being, where did he originate, and what power does he really possess?

When we think of Satan — the devil — we often conjure up a picture of a man with horns and a tail, dressed in a red suit, carrying a pitchfork. We picture him presiding over the fires of Hades, welcoming each new arrival with a diabolical grin, and deciding what sort of horrendous torture would fit that newly arrived and eternally damned inmate.

He would have cloven hooves instead of normal feet, perhaps wearing a thin mustache, and look something like Simon Legree when he tied Little Eva to the railroad track as the train approached.

This somewhat comical figure is *exactly* what Satan would like us to believe he is, but he is not like that at all. He is in no way a "funny little man" in red leotards, an innocuous and amusing creature who can be laughed at. He is correctly described in 1 Peter 5:8, "Be sober, be vigilant; because your adversary the devil, as a roaring lion, walketh about, seeking whom he may devour." Be careful of Satan, for he is dangerous. Just ask Adam and Eve.

Satan can be quite charming and persuasive. He can appear as a very beautiful person, flattering us with lies, and expertly exploiting our weaknesses — which he knows intimately. His arguments may seem logical, but they contain a poison which is toxic and lethal to our souls. Many times we are not aware that it is Satan whispering in our ear until it is too late. It is not until then that we realize who has been softly encouraging us, and we find that we have responded to the voice of the destroyer.

Satan is referred to in the Bible over one hundred times. The name *Satan* comes from a Hebrew word meaning adversary, enemy, or accuser. Translated into Greek, Satan becomes Diabolos, from which we get the term "devil." In the Bible he is also called Beelzebub, Belial, the Great Dragon, the Serpent, the tempter, and Day Star — which is translated Lucifer in the King James Version. Custom, folklore, and tradition have ascribed many other names to Satan in various parts of the world — but he is known universally. Every religion on earth has a counterpart to the Satan of the Bible. He has been a very busy traveler.

But just who is this creature we call Satan? Where did he come from? What are his powers? Should Christians really fear him? Let us examine the facts and find the answers to these questions.

Satan's Former Position in Heaven

The prophet Ezekiel, under God's anointing, writes some strange things in chapter 28 of his book. Although his statements are apparently directed against the prince of an earthly kingdom, Tyrus, what he says can pertain only to someone who is not a typical, mortal, man. He tells us about Tyrus in Ezekiel 28:13: "Thou hast been in Eden the garden of God; every precious stone was thy covering, the sardis, topaz, and the diamond, the beryl, the onyx, and the jasper, the sapphire, the emerald, and the carbuncle, and gold: the workmanship of thy tabrets and thy pipes was prepared in the day that thou wast created."

From this point it is evident that this prince, Tyrus, to whom Ezekiel's message is directed, is a *created* being, and not an earthly, human prince. This creature had been in the Garden of Eden, and from the Bible we know that only Adam, Eve, and Satan were in that garden. Since Ezekiel's statements are obviously not directed to either Adam or Eve, that leaves only one creature, one created creature — Satan — to whom Ezekiel is speaking.

The next verses amplify that position: "Thou art the anointed cherub that covereth; and I have set thee so: thou wast upon the holy mountain of God; thou hast walked up and down in the midst of the stones of fire. Thou wast perfect in thy ways from the day that thou wast created, till iniquity was found in thee" (Ezek. 28:14-15).

No mortal man could have been the anointed cherub which had covered God's throne. No mere man could have walked in the midst of the stones of fire which are a part of it — as Ezekiel saw in his vision described in Ezekiel 1:4. No man walked on God's holy mountain. Only one very special created being could be described here — the cherub who covered the Most High with his golden wings as God sat upon His throne.

What does Ezekiel say happened to this covering cherub, this most beautiful creature who formerly occupied a very special place in heaven? "Therefore I will cast thee as profane out of the mountain of God: and I will destroy thee, O covering cherub, from the midst of the stones of fire" (Ezek. 28:16).

What happened to change this perfect and marvelously formed cherub? What did he do to provoke such terrible wrath from God? "Thine heart was lifted up because of thy beauty, thou hast corrupted thy wisdom by reason of thy brightness" (Ezek. 28:17).

Satan had occupied at one time the highest and most cherished position in heaven. He had been God's covering cherub, the most beautiful creature ever created, adorned with vestments covered with precious stones.

But Satan, the covering cherub, was not content with his high place in heaven. He was so impressed with his own beauty, his own intellect, his own power, all of which were *gifts* given to him by his Creator — that he imagined himself above God. He conspired to depose and take the place of the very One who had created him. Satan was so persuasive that he actually convinced one-third of the angels in heaven to join his rebellion. We know from this that even the angels have a *free will* and are capable of deciding whom they will follow: God or Satan. Man must make this very same decision.

We also have a free will, capable of making a choice between good and evil. We can choose to rebel against God, as Satan did. But just as Satan did not succeed, we cannot succeed. Just as Satan must pay the price of rebellion, so must we pay a price — a very high price. Just as God's wrath was directed against Satan, it can be directed against us. We are free to make this choice — but we, like Satan, must eventually suffer the consequences of that choice.

In the vision which John received on the Isle of Patmos, he beheld what happened when Satan led this revolt against God.

The War in Heaven

We on earth measure time by our own experience. A day to us is the revolution of our planet once on its axis. A year is a complete journey of our earth around the sun. Our reference to the passing of time is limited by our own circumstance of being a passenger on this insignificant speck of rock as it travels in the infinity of space, tied by forces of gravity to a star which is part of a galaxy of billions of other stars.

God, on the other hand, is not limited by these purely physical reference points for what we call time. It is very difficult, therefore, when we read the Scriptures, to determine just when some events take place, especially in the spiritual realm of God's unlimited concept of what we call time. The war in heaven is just such an event.

John, the Revelator, tells us in Revelation 12:7-9, "And there was war in heaven: Michael and his angels fought against the dragon; and the dragon fought and his angels, And prevailed not; neither was their place found any more in heaven. And the great dragon was cast out, that old serpent, called the Devil, and Satan, which deceiveth the whole world: he was cast out into the earth, and his angels were cast out with him."

We are, perhaps, given some insight on the time when this took place, for in the previous verses we are told of the birth of Jesus, His being taken up to God's throne, and the persecution of the woman who had given birth to him. Certainly, by the death on the cross and His resurrection, Jesus Christ defeated Satan.

We are warned of what Satan's being cast out of heaven into the earth will mean for us: "Woe to the inhabiters of the earth and the sea! for the devil is come down unto you, having great wrath, because he knoweth that he hath but a short time" (Rev. 12:12).

In Luke 10:18 Jesus also gives us an insight in His own words, ". . . I beheld Satan as lightning fall from heaven."

The Book of Revelation informs us of Satan's final destruction after Jesus Christ returns to earth in power and glory, to also defeat the forces of the Antichrist. But until that time, Satan is loose upon this planet, deceiving men in the manner in which he deceived God's angels — and causing the eternal destruction of the souls of men and women just as the fallen angels are destined to spend eternity in the lake of unquenchable fire.

We know that Satan was at one time in the highest position in heaven before he rebelled against God. We know that he had been in the Garden of Eden to tempt Eve and cause the fall of man into sin. What was his role between the time he lost his privileged position as the anointed cherub and his defeat by Jesus Christ on the cross at Calvary and His Resurrection from the tomb?

Job gives us some very interesting insight on just what Satan was up to during that time, and we will also learn the limits of his power.

Satan — The Accuser before God

Job 1:7 states, "Now there was a day when the sons of God came to present themselves before the Lord, and Satan came also among them. And the Lord said unto Satan, Whence comest thou? Then Satan answered the Lord, and said, From going to and fro in the earth, and from walking up and down in it."

It is apparent that at this time Satan was allowed to enter heaven and go before the throne of God. Although through Satan's seduction of Eve, evil and sin had come upon the earth, the Tempter was free to go back and forth between heaven and earth. What was Satan's purpose before the throne of God?

The Lord then drew Satan's attention to a particular man on earth whose name was Job, a righteous man. "Hast thou considered my servant Job, that there is none like him in the earth, a perfect and an upright man, one that feareth God, and escheweth evil?" (Job 1:8).

Job was not only a righteous man, but a wealthy and prosperous one, as well. He owned large herds of cattle and many flocks of sheep. Job had much in the way of material goods. And although Job lived near the land of the Sabeans who often raided and plundered innocent herders and farmers, God had kept him safe from these fierce tribesmen.

Satan answered God with a question: "Doth Job fear God for naught? Hast not thou made an hedge about him, and about his house, and about all that he hath on every side? thou hast blessed the work of his hands, and his substance is increased in the land" (Job 1:10).

Then Satan brought an accusation against Job, and a challenge for God: "But put forth thine hand now, and touch all that he hath, and he will curse thee to thy face" (Job 1:11).

What Satan was implying was that Job was a righteous man *because* God had blessed him. Satan accused Job of fearing God in order to gain the riches that he had amassed, and not for any other reason. Satan challenged God to remove the hedge of protection around Job, to take away his material substance — and then to see if Job would still revere God. Satan accused Job of being righteous only for what it got him in material possessions.

God accepted this challenge. He allowed Satan to bring hardship and poverty upon Job. The rest of the Book of Job tells of Job's spiritual struggle, his eventual victory, and the restoration of all his wealth. God had faith in Job, and Job did not let Him down.

What we see here is Satan's role after his rebellion and after God had removed him from his high position as covering cherub. Satan was the accuser, the one who brought charges against God's people on earth. In Revelation 12:10 we find confirmation of this, and Satan's defeat by Jesus Christ, "... for the accuser of our brethren is cast down, which accused them before our God day and night."

Just as he has been brought down, Satan wants to bring others down with him. But the story of Job gives us another insight — what Satan's real powers are — and their limits.

Satan's Power

Satan could not touch Job until God had given him permission to do so. Why? Because Job was a righteous man and God had put a hedge around him. Only God — and Job himself, could remove that hedge. Satan could not go through it until either God said he could, or Job had torn it down himself by turning away from God. There is a lesson for Christians here which is very important.

God referred to Job as *His* servant. Christians of today are God's servants on earth — if they give their lives to Jesus Christ and lead the type of righteous life that Job led. Just as God placed an impenetrable hedge around Job, God will place a hedge around His servants today. But the problem with many Christians is that they fear the power of Satan *more* than they trust the power of God to protect them. We tear down that hedge by doubt, by not trusting God in *everything*, and by doing exactly what Satan wants us to do — not placing our lives and future completely in God's hands.

Satan's ultimate desire is to be worshipped. But if he cannot achieve that, he will settle for being feared. When Christians take their eyes off of Jesus Christ and start thinking too much about Satan, then bad things begin to happen in their lives. When we, ourselves, let down that hedge, we allow Satan's power to touch us. Far too many Christians, when God allows adversity to confront us in order to strengthen our faith, attribute this to the work of the devil, and run and hide instead of placing our total and absolute trust in God to bring us through difficult times — and strengthen our faith.

Satan *does* have power on earth. In 2 Corinthians 4:4 Paul refers to him as the "god of this world." Those who slip out from under the protective hedge of God are open to his destruction. He brings his deception in many forms: dishonesty, illegal drugs, alcohol abuse, sexual perversion, adultery, promiscuity, lust for wealth, power or social status, or whatever our weakness may be. He presents these to the vulnerable as desirable and fulfilling, but those who are deceived by his lies are destroyed. Remember, Satan fell — and he wants to bring all men and women down with him into the pit.

We have a full set of armor to wear against him, but don't allow even a tiny crack to develop in that armor — for he can wriggle through the smallest opening. Paul, in Ephesians 6:13-17 tells us what our armor consists of: gird your loins with truth, wear the breastplate of righteousness, the shoes of the gospel of peace, take hold of the shield of faith, put on the helmet of salvation, and arm yourself with the sword of the spirit — the Word of God.

Even the disciples of Jesus were not immune from letting down their guard. When Simon Peter rebuked Jesus after He told them that He must be put to death at Jerusalem, Jesus said to Peter, "Get thee behind me, Satan...." Jesus addressed Peter, but His words were for Satan, who had entered the disciple through a crack in Peter's spiritual armor. Again, after what we call the Last Supper, Jesus said to Peter, "Simon, Simon, behold,

Satan hath desired to have you, that he may sift you as wheat." If even Simon Peter, who had been the first one to declare that Jesus was the Son of God, whom Jesus had named "Cephas" which means in Aramaic, *stone,* who had been with the Master for over three years and witnessed countless miracles, was not totally immune to Satan's deception — can you imagine the state of the average Christian today?

But after all this, Peter, on the night of Jesus' trial before the Jewish leaders — denied *three times* that he even knew Jesus. Take hope, for after the Resurrection, Peter actually became the *rock* of faith, as the Master had named him.

Christian Persecution

There is a difference between being vulnerable to Satan's attacks, and being persecuted for your faith. Christians are not of this world, and can expect persecution to come from those who are of this world. Jesus told us to be ready for this. "If ye were of the world, the world would love his own: but because ye are not of the world, but I have chosen you out of the world, therefore the world hateth you. Remember the word that I said unto you, The servant is not greater than his lord. If they have persecuted me, they will also persecute you..." (John 15:19-20).

When you become a Christian you are *no longer of this world.* Therefore you are different from those of this world. Expect to face persecution from those who *are* of this world.

Now I want to make something perfectly clear: If you are a strong Christian working diligently for the Lord you will be a target of Satan's attack. He is the "god of this world," and you will be an alien in it. Those who are no threat to him, he usually leaves alone. After all, they already *belong* to him.

Apparently many in the early Church were bewildered and confused when hardship and persecution came upon them. Peter tried to reassure them. In 1 Peter 4:16 he told them, "Yet if any man suffer as a Christian, let him not be ashamed; but let him glorify God on this behalf."

Satan will attack the area in our lives where we are most vulnerable: our marriages, children, jobs, self-esteem, and health. If you are truly working for the Lord, expect this and, as Peter tells us, do not be dismayed. Count it a blessing that you have been considered such a strong enemy of Satan that you have been chosen as a target of his attack. Wear your armor, keep your faith, and God will bring you through whatever Satan throws at you.

One thing we must *never* do when we come under attack is to turn and run. If we examine the spiritual armor Paul talks about, we find that all of it is in the *front*. There is no armor covering our rear. If we turn and run, there is no protective shield covering us — and Satan's darts can wound us terribly. In James 4:7 we are told how to deal with Satan when he attacks: "Resist the devil, and he will flee from you."

What Is Satan's Kingdom?

After Jesus had been baptized by John, He went into the wilderness forty days to be tempted by the devil. "And the devil, taking him up into an high mountain, shewed unto him all the kingdoms of the world in a moment of time. And the devil said unto him, All this power will I give thee, and the glory of them: for that is delivered unto me; and to whomsoever I will give it" (Luke 4:5-6).

The world is the kingdom of Satan, but he has been given only temporary dominion over it. The nations of this world belong to him, along with their riches and power. He has the authority to share their power and wealth with anyone he chooses.

But this authority will not last forever. When the crowds were about Jesus in the days just prior to His crucifixion, He told them Satan's power over the earth would not be forever. "Now is the judgment of this world: now shall the prince of this world be cast out" (John 12:31).

A few days later Jesus gave His life on the cross, and three days later arose in victory over death. He defeated Satan and brought the kingdom of God to the earth. The battle between these kingdoms has raged ever since.

Satan tried his best to destroy the early Christian church. By placing men of his own choosing in positions of power in the Roman Empire, he attempted to wipe out the believers in Jesus Christ. First Caligula, then Nero and later emperors persecuted and killed Christians. But the more vicious the attacks of Satan, the more solid became the faith and determination of the early Christians. Satan did not succeed in destroying Christianity, but he is still trying. Only his tactics have changed.

Where he was not successful in physically destroying the

faithful of the early church, he is, unfortunately, succeeding in destroying many today spiritually. Many Christian denominations have now watered down their faith to a point where it is virtually nonexistent. Many of our seminaries have become spiritual cemeteries for young people, where professors of theology deny the virgin birth, the Resurrection, and the very person of Jesus Christ as the Son of God. Some biblical scholars question whether the Scriptures are really valid in today's society. Some even declare them to be forgeries, written much later in time.

What Satan could not accomplish from *outside* the Christian church, he is accomplishing from *within* the church itself.

But, thank God, there remain those who have not compromised the faith, have held to God's Word, and have resisted the efforts of those who would change Christianity to please men rather than change men to please God.

Paul writes in 2 Thessalonians 2:3 about a great "falling away" which would occur before the Lord returned. In order to fall away, one must have been part of something to begin with. What we are witnessing today, I believe, is that falling away of believers in preparation for the return of Jesus Christ, just as Paul said there would be.

Is Satan Lord of Hell?

Since hell is a holding place for the unrighteous until they face final judgment, it was neither created by, nor is it presided over, by Satan. For him to be in charge of hell would be like having Charles Manson in charge of a maximum security prison. At the Great White Throne judgment, Satan, hell, and death will be cast into the lake of fire, along with the angels who followed him in rebellion against God — and all whose names are not written in the Book of Life. You can read about this in Revelation 20:10,14,15, and in Matthew 25:41.

It is apparent from Scripture that Satan's kingdom is not hell, but this world. The kingdom of God is not of *this* world, and if Christians try to live too much in this world they are leaving themselves wide open to Satan's influence in their lives.

Conclusions about Satan

From what we have learned from God's Word about Satan and his power, we can draw some conclusions about who he is and what he can and cannot do:

- Satan is a being which God created in heaven.
- He existed before God created the earth and Adam and Eve.
- He was not just an ordinary angel, but the covering cherub above the throne of God.
- He was the most beautiful and gifted of all created beings in heaven.
- He had a free will, capable of obeying or rebelling against God.
- He chose to rebel and persuaded one-third of the angels to join him.
- Satan and his angels were cast out of heaven to earth.
- Satan was given authority over the kingdoms of the earth.
- He can give this authority to those he chooses.
- He cannot touch the righteous without God's permission.
- He can make sin appear beautiful to those he deceives.
- He is a liar and will twist God's Word from Scripture.
- Satan was the accuser of men before the throne of God.
- He will attack Christians if they let down their guard.
- He has already been defeated by Jesus Christ.

A Final Word about Satan

Many Christians today blame all their problems and troubles on Satan. Although it is true that he will try to prevent believers from doing the Lord's work on earth in any way he can, he is certainly not responsible for all of our personal difficulties.

We cannot escape the responsibility for our own shortcomings and failures by stating, as Flip Wilson's favorite character always said, "The devil made me do it!" Most often, the devil didn't do it; we bring most of our problems on ourselves.

We must remember to keep our eyes focused on Jesus Christ, and not Satan. The primary mission of Christians is to bring as many lost souls into God's kingdom as possible, and Satan will try his best to divert us from this. When Satan is the object of our attention, we can accomplish very little.

12

Manna from Heaven — What Was It?

For many people, especially those with a scientific background, the miracles described in the Bible are a stumbling block for faith. Even young people who have been raised in an excellent Christian atmosphere and have received Bible training since their early days begin to find doubts creeping into their minds at the high school and college levels of their education, because what they are being taught in school runs completely counter to any belief in miracles.

One of these hard to reconcile miracles is described in Exodus 16:4: "Then said the Lord unto Moses, Behold, I will rain bread from heaven for you; and the people shall go out and gather a certain rate every day...."

"Bread from heaven? How could this be possible?" the skeptics ask. For them it is just another reason to dismiss *all* of what the Bible says as myth, superstition, and nonsense. Countless people have been turned away from salvation from incidents such as this one contained in the Bible.

But is this an impossibility? This book would not be complete without a scientific look at what *may* have happened in the wilderness to produce the manna, the "bread from heaven" which fed the Israelites.

First, I want to say that I certainly believe that God is capable of performing miracles. I have been the recipient of more than one. I also believe that He can, and often does, use natural forces and events in a supernatural way to perform some of them. With this in mind, and taking *nothing* away from

God's ability to do anything He desires to do, let's look at what *might* have happened to produce the manna.

The Israelites had been in Egypt for four hundred and thirty years. The family of Jacob had numbered seventy when he had brought them into Egypt to escape the famine, but during the course of over four centuries they had grown into a nation. But for much of this time they had been slaves to the Egyptians and their lives had been hard. As difficult as life may have been, however, the Israelites had not gone hungry. The fertile land along the Nile had provided amply for them. But now, after Moses had led them into the wilderness, they looked about them and saw no fields of wheat or vegetables, no juicy melons or spicy onions. "What are we going to eat?" they complained to one another.

They confronted Moses and Aaron. "Would to God we had died by the hand of the Lord in the land of Egypt, when we sat by the flesh pots, and when we did eat bread to the full; for ye have brought us forth into this wilderness, to kill this whole assembly with hunger" (Exod. 16:3).

Just about a month before, they had witnessed firsthand the power of God when He had parted the waters and allowed them to cross on dry land, then watched as the waters destroyed the army of Pharaoh which had pursued them. What short memories! Certainly, if God could do this, then He could also provide whatever they needed to sustain them. But human nature being what it is, would we have reacted any differently?

It is important to note that they were in a *wilderness* and not a desert. There is a huge difference. This was not the Sahara, where endless sand dunes stretch with no vegetation. This was the Wilderness of Sin, which was quite different, with scrub grass and low growing brush, and even some small trees here and there. True, there was little water, but Bedouins have lived and survived in this wilderness for thousands of years.

But the Israelites did not possess the survival skills of the Bedouins. After over four hundred years of Egyptian captivity, they had become accustomed to an entirely different way of life. Suddenly uprooted from their former existence as slaves, where decisions were made for them by their Egyptian overlords, they could neither think for themselves nor function as yet as free men. All they could see was starvation in this wilderness, and they were terrified.

God knew this and was prepared to feed them. He would supply them every morning with food which would appear mysteriously on the ground and occasionally with the meat of quail which would drop out of the sky in the evening. These events certainly have all the aspects of being unexplainable miracles. But are they? Let's see what may have happened.

The time was the spring of the year. For eons birds have migrated from the coming, unbearable heat of Africa to the cooler climate of Europe. There are two major migratory routes, one of which crosses the Red Sea and the eastern Mediterranean. Quail are among the birds which follow this route. These birds must travel long distances across water, and when they approach the shores of the Red Sea they are physically spent. Bedouins gather these exhausted birds as they lay almost helpless after this extended flight.

The migratory flight path takes birds today over the exact location where the Israelites would have been when Moses led them out of Egypt. Since migratory routes seldom change, we have every reason to expect that the quail, in the early months of the year of the Exodus, would have also followed that route. "And the Lord spake unto Moses, saying, I have heard the murmurings of the children of Israel: speak unto them, saying, At even ye shall eat flesh, and in the morning ye shall be filled with bread; and ye shall know that I am the Lord your God" (Exod. 16:11-12).

The day passed and evening approached as the Israelites watched apprehensively. Then it happened. Birds began to fall from the sky. "And it came to pass, that at even the quails came up, and covered the camp . . . ." (Exod. 16:13). Is the power of God lessened because of the fact that this was caused by the exhaustion of quail on their annual migratory flight from Africa to Europe? I think not. God, in His infinite wisdom, had anticipated the reaction of the Israelites. Days or even weeks before, He had caused an enormous flock of quail to begin their migratory flight north. Then, at the precise time the Israelites had complained about the lack of food, they had begun their long flight over the waters of the sea, arriving that very evening to collapse in exhaustion in the camp of the children of Israel. Even though God may have used something as natural as the annual migration of these birds to feed His people, His timing of their arrival cannot be called less than a miracle.

Manna — the Bread from Heaven

But what about the manna? Can this also be explained as simply as the arrival of the quail?

The next morning the Israelites looked out on a strange sight. The ground was covered with something white. "And when the dew that lay was gone up, behold, upon the face of the wilderness there lay a small round thing, as small as the hoar frost on the ground" (Exod. 16:14).

They didn't have the slightest idea what this white stuff was. "And when the children of Israel saw it, they said one to another, It is manna: for they wist not what it was. And Moses said unto them, This is the bread which the Lord has given you to eat" (Exod. 16:15).

When they saw it they said, "It is *man-hu*." In Hebrew, this is the same as asking the question, "What is this?" So that's what they called it. The bread of heaven was called manna, or in Hebrew, "What's this stuff?"

They tasted it. "And it was like coriander seed, white; and the taste of it was like wafers made with honey" (Exod. 16:31).

We are told a few more things about manna. If the Israelites did not get out and collect it before the sun came up and it became hot, the manna "melted." We are also told that Moses instructed the people not to gather any more than they required for the day, and not to try to keep it overnight. Some of the people disregarded this order and placed the manna in pots to keep it for the next day. We are told that it "bred worms and stank."

Only on the day before the Sabbath were the Israelites allowed to gather a two day's supply, and Moses instructed them how to prepare it to keep it from spoiling.

But what was this manna? Did it really drop from the sky, as snow does, to feed these people? Can we find another possible explanation, using some natural occurrence similar to migrating quail, to explain manna?

Yes, I believe we can. This also does not take away anything from the power of God, as you will see.

We have said previously that the wilderness was not a desert. Grass, brush, and small trees grew although not in as great profusion as along the Nile in Egypt. One of these low growing scrub trees is the tamarisk

There is a small beetle which lives on tamarisks and when

this beetle pierces the tree, it exudes a resin which then drips to the ground. As it solidifies it becomes white in color. The drippings of resin are about the size and shape of a coriander seed. When tasted, it is very sweet — similar to the taste of honey. These white "wafers" disappear when the sun comes up and the day becomes hot. It does not melt, but it is the food of choice of the swarms of ants which inhabit this area. These insects are dormant during the chill of the night, but when the sun's rays warm up the ground they become extremely active and in no time all of the resin has been consumed.

Does this sound plausible? Could this resin which drips from the twigs and branches of the tamarisk really be the same as the manna that the children of Israel ate? Would there be sufficient quantity of it?

In 1483 and eyewitness account was written by a visitor to the area, Breitenbach, Dean of Mainz, after visiting the Sinai. "In every valley throughout the whole region of Mt. Sinai there still can be found Bread of Heaven, which the monks and Arabs gather, preserve, and sell to pilgrims and strangers who pass that way. This same Bread of Heaven falls about daybreak like dew or hoarfrost and hangs in beads on grass, stones, and twigs. It is sweet like honey and sticks to the teeth. We bought a lot of it."[1]

Botanists from the Hebrew University in Jerusalem have confirmed that this "manna" is still to be found in the Sinai all the way up to the Dead Sea. They established the fact that the beetles cause the small trees to exude a resin which drips down onto whatever is below. It's appearance is white in color, turning yellow-brown after lying around for some time. "The taste is particularly sweet," they reported. "It is most of all like honey when it has been left for a long time to solidify."

Arab merchants still sell jars and bottles of *Mann es-Sama* to tourists. They gather it from beneath the tamarisks before the sun is very high in the morning while the ants are dormant. I saw it being sold in Arab stalls on a recent trip to the Middle East. I must confess that I did not taste it, for the containers it was being sold in didn't look very clean. I was told that a man could collect several pounds quite easily and rapidly in the morning, enough to satisfy his hunger for that day, at least.

Is this what the Israelites ate in the Wilderness of Sin? It certainly appears that it could have been. Does this take anything away from God's power to perform miracles? No, I don't think so. They needed food and God provided the food. Incidentally, if you don't seal the jars containing Mann es-Sama, which means "bread from heaven," the ants get into it. By the next morning it looks sort of wormy and is completely spoiled.

13

The Jordan Parted —
Myth or Miracle?

When the Hebrews left their bondage in Egypt, God parted the waters to allow them to escape Pharaoh's army. Now, forty years later, they were prepared to enter the land that He had promised them. Again they faced a body of water, the Jordan River. Although the river was fairly narrow, the waters were swift and the current much too fast for them to wade across.

Much had happened to this people in forty years. They had left Egypt as newly freed slaves, a disorganized horde, incapable of thinking for themselves, and lacking in spiritual courage. Under God's direction, Moses had made all decisions for them. When they had complained, he had settled their grievances. After they had angered God by rebellion, it had been Moses who pleaded their case for forgiveness. When they disobeyed, it was Moses who disciplined them.

The Lord had given them His laws. He had engraved His Ten Commandments upon stone tablets, and His ordinances controlled almost every aspect of their daily lives. God had fed them and protected them, tested and hardened them, rebuked and chastened them. Now, the rabble which had left Egypt with a slave mentality had passed away and their children had been forged on the anvil of the wilderness by the iron hammer of God into a mighty nation.

At last they were ready to enter into this new land, *their* land which God had promised to them as descendents of Abraham. But Moses would no longer lead them.

Moses, perhaps the greatest of the Old Testament prophets,

the man who had spoken with God face to face, was not above the reproach and punishment of God. When the Lord had instructed him to *speak* to a certain rock to obtain water, Moses had disobeyed and had *struck* the rock with his rod. Perhaps God could have forgiven this, but Moses — with an uncharacteristic burst of spiritual pride — had shouted to the unruly Hebrews, "Hear now, ye rebels; must *we* fetch you water out of this rock?" (Num. 20:10).

In using the plural pronoun "we," Moses was placing *himself* on an equal footing with God in performing this miracle. It was for this offence that he would not be allowed to enter the Promised Land.

So when the time came to cross the Jordan into Canaan, it was time for Moses to die and a new leader to be chosen. But God did allow Moses to see this land, and Moses climbed to the top of Mt. Nebo where he could gaze across the river. From this mountain he could see far to the north, beyond the Sea of Galilee to the snowcapped peak of Mt. Hermon. To the east and the south, as far as his eyes could see, were the red-brown hills and desert, and to the west was the blue of the Mediterranean Sea. All that Moses' tear-filled eyes could see, the Lord was giving to His chosen people.

He stood there gazing out upon this land until the Lord said that it was time. "So Moses, the servant of the Lord, died there in the land of Moab, according to the word of the Lord. And he buried him in a valley in the land of Moab, over against Bethpeor: but no man knoweth of his sepulchre unto this day" (Deut. 34:5-6).

There was a good reason for God to bury Moses in a secret place. The Hebrews already were carrying the bones of Joseph with them, to bury them in Canaan. Moses, being their spiritual leader for forty years, would certainly have been provided with a splendid tomb, a place where they would have come to pay homage to their great leader. In time, the sepulchre of Moses would have become a religious shrine, and God wanted no man to be worshipped in His place. Apparently it was Michael, the archangel, who physically buried Moses, for in Jude 9 we are told, "Yet Michael the archangel when contending with the devil he disputed about the body of Moses . . . ." Satan, of course, would have liked to have had Moses' burial place known so that the site could become a shrine revered by the Hebrews.

Joshua Chosen

Of the men of the generation which had left Egypt with Moses, only two remained alive as they faced the crossing of the Jordan River into Canaan. These two men had been part of the group sent into Canaan to spy out the land shortly after leaving Egypt. But of all the spies, only Joshua and Caleb had been willing to trust the Lord and immediately enter this land. The rest of the spies, fearful of the unknown, had brought back reports of giants and fierce tribesmen.

Joshua had become Moses' right hand man, and was a proven and dependable leader. Now that Moses was dead, the mantle of leadership fell upon his broad and capable shoulders. Moses had consecrated him, with the approval of the Lord, to take his place and lead Israel into the Promised Land.

It would not be an easy task. Across the Jordan stood the fortress city of Jericho. It would have to be taken, for it guarded the gateway into Canaan. Joshua knew that only with the Lord's help could this be accomplished.

But God had assured him of that help. Joshua 1:5 tells us of the Lord's promise to him: "There shall not any man be able to stand before thee all the days of thy life: as I was with Moses, so shall I be with thee: I will not fail thee, nor forsake thee."

The Israelites grieved thirty days for Moses, and at the end of that time Joshua prepared to cross the Jordan River not far from the fortress of the city of Jericho. The time had come to take possession of the land which God had promised to the children of Abraham.

The Jordan

The Jordan River flows through a geological area which is part of the Great Rift Valley. This extended fault line begins in Africa and runs through the Middle East all the way north to eastern Turkey. It is a seismically active area where earthquakes are common, and earth tremors occur frequently. The Dead Sea was formed when the floor of this part of the Great Rift Valley tilted to the south and plunged below sea level during a seismic upheaval.

From the beginning of the Jordan River in Lebanon and Syria, the river drops 696 feet in elevation on its course to the Sea of Galilee, then drops an additional 596 feet to where it discharges its water into the Dead Sea. It is a swift-flowing river, and very difficult to cross during the spring when the rains and the melting snow of Mt. Hermon adds torrents of water to its flow. During the dry summer, a few places exist where it is possible to wade across, and several fords have been found which were used before bridges were built. But when the Hebrews prepared to enter Canaan, it was spring — and the Jordan was overflowing its banks. Fording this river was out of the question. But God had already planned for this and was again to demonstrate His power.

Because of the narrow width of the Jordan and the high cliffs along much of its banks, occasionally it becomes temporarily dammed up by slides of rock and soil. Even a fairly minor earth tremor can cause this to happen. There are many recent instances when the Jordan's flow has been stopped for a short time and similar occurrences have been recorded going back as far as A.D. 1267.[1]

As Joshua contemplated how he was to get this huge number of people safely across the swollen river, the Lord spoke to him: "Now therefore take you twelve men out of the tribes of Israel, out of every tribe a man. And it shall come to pass, as soon as the soles of the feet of the priests that bear the ark of the Lord, the Lord of all the earth, shall rest in the waters of Jordan, that the waters of Jordan shall be cut off from the waters that come down from above, and they shall stand upon a heap" (Josh. 3:12-13).

The key word to the understanding of what happened is the word *heap*. The dictionary defines this word as "a pile, mass, or mound of things jumbled together."[2] This describes a dam, which would have been caused by a landslide of dirt and rock, and would have cut off the flow of water in the Jordan.

In Joshua 3:16 we are given additional evidence that this is indeed what happened. "That the waters which came down from above stood and rose up upon a heap very far from the city of Adam, that is beside Zaretan: and those that came down toward the sea of the plain, even the salt sea, failed, and were cut off: and the people passed over right against Jericho."

Archaeologists have placed Zaretan about twenty-five miles north of Jericho. Adamah, the city of Adam, was near the existing town of Damya, where the Damia bridge now crosses the Jordan. The archaeological site is known as Tell es-Saidiyeh and lies on the eastern side of the Jordan about halfway between where the river flows out of the Sea of

Galilee and where it empties into the Dead Sea.

Did a Miracle Occur Here?

The fact that God used an earth tremor to cause a slide of rock and dirt to temporarily block the flow of water in the Jordan River, just as He caused a strong wind to part the waters which allowed the Hebrews to escape Pharaoh's army in Egypt, does not in the least diminish the miracle which occurred here. The precise timing of the minor earthquake which caused the slide points indisputably to the fact that God is in complete control of the *natural* occurrences on the earth as well as the supernatural.

Imagine, a timing so exact that as soon as the soles of the priest's feet touched the water, the flow of the river ceased. This is most certainly an "unnatural" event, although the water was dammed upstream by what the world would call a "natural" cause. Just as Jesus commanded the wind and the waves to be calm, and these natural phenomena obeyed Him, the Lord was in total and complete control of the natural events which caused the flow of water in the Jordan River to be impounded by a dam caused by a precisely timed earth tremor. It was, without a shadow of a doubt, a miracle.

The Spiritual Significance

On God's orders, Joshua had twelve stones removed out of the riverbed and carried to the other side in Canaan. These were set up as a memorial. Also, twelve additional stones were set up in the midst of the river, at the place where the priests who carried the ark of the covenant had stood as the Israelites passed over. Can we find any significance in the placing of these two sets of twelve stones, one across the river, and one in the midst of it? Yes, there is a tremendous significance in these memorials.

The full spiritual significance would not be realized until Jesus began His ministry well over a thousand years later and He came to the Jordan to be baptized by John. We do not know the exact location where this occurred, but it may have been at or very close to where the Israelites crossed the Jordan and these stone memorials had been set up. When John questioned Jesus' need to be baptized, His reply is recorded in Matthew 3:15: "Suffer it to be so now: for thus it becometh us to fulfil all righteousness."

Let us examine what baptism signifies and compare it to the

two sets of stones left by Joshua as a memorial: one in the midst of the water and one on the bank of the river in the Promised Land. When a person is immersed in the baptismal water it signifies the "death of the old person," leaving behind in the water all past sins. The stones left by Joshua in the midst of the Jordan signified the death of "old Israel," and the leaving behind of all of their past transgressions.

When a person comes up from the baptismal water he is a "new creation," a redeemed soul, totally forgiven, and entering into a new life of hope and promise. This is what the nation of Israel entered into as they passed through Jordan and entered into the land which was their hope and promise from God. Although they did not realize this at the time, these two sets of stone memorials were signifying their baptism, and they were actually partaking of the coming death and resurrection of Jesus Christ as they passed through the waters of Jordan.

The Covenant Renewed

After they had entered Canaan, and before they proceeded to Jericho, the Lord gave Joshua another command: "Make thee sharp knives, and circumcise again the children of Israel the second time. And Joshua made him sharp knives, and circumcised the children of Israel at the hill of the foreskins" (Josh. 5:2-3).

On that day God renewed the Covenant He had made with Abraham with the generation that was to realize those Covenant promises. They had been forged as a nation in the wilderness, now they were to take possession of the land which God had sworn to give to them. No longer Egyptian slaves, they were a free people. "And the Lord said unto Joshua, This day have I rolled away the reproach of Egypt from off you. Wherefore the name of the place is called Gilgal unto this day" (Josh. 5:9).

Gilgal literally means "a rolling." Uncircumcised, the Israelites did not have the sign of God's covenant which He had made with Abraham over five centuries before. Now, with this sign and with all the reproach of Egypt rolled from off their backs, they were at last ready to take physical possession of the land and receive the full blessing of the promises.

Was the stopping of the waters of Jordan truly a miracle? Yes, it was. But it was also a foreshadow of a greater miracle to come — one in which all of us have a part — the death and resurrection of the Lord Jesus Christ.

14

Did the Walls of Jericho Really Fall Down?

After crossing the Jordan River the Israelites camped at a location which was named Gilgal. It was early spring and the nearby fields were heavy with grain planted by the Canaanites months before. Jericho is located in a semi-tropical area, and crops may be grown almost year round. The Israelites ate of the bounty of these fields, which the Bible calls the "old corn."

This was not corn as we know it, but cereal grains such as wheat and barley. With no more need of manna, God no longer provided the "Bread of Heaven" to feed them. Of course, they were out of the region where the tamarisk grew in great profusion.

Joshua 5:10 tells us that they celebrated Passover on the fourteenth day of Nisan in the plains of Jericho. Just five miles away stood the fortified city of Jericho which must be captured for them to successfully enter the land of Canaan, for it was the guardian of the eastern entrance of the central hill country. Any invader must first reduce or capture this heavily walled city before entering Canaan. The Bible tells us that Joshua went personally to look over the task that lay before him.

Jericho is one of the oldest inhabited sites in history, with signs of occupation dating back eight thousand years. Being 670 feet below sea level, it is also the world's lowest city. Many times in the past it had been confronted with invading armies. Many had been successfully repelled, a few had breached its walls. But the protecting battlements of stone and mud-brick must have appeared almost impregnable to Joshua as he surveyed them from below.

As Joshua observed from his hiding place, sentries manned the low towers atop the wall, peering out onto the plains for any sign of attack. They were well aware that the Israelites had crossed the Jordan and were now camped just a few miles away. The spies which Joshua had sent into the city had first alarmed them and they were expecting an assault upon their city at any time. The farmers who lived outside the walls had withdrawn within them, the food storage bins in the city were full to overflowing in preparation for an extended siege, the water cisterns were full. Jericho was ready and waiting for the attack.

As Joshua peered intently at the walls of Jericho, looking for any sign of weakness in the defense, he was suddenly startled by the appearance of a man standing close to him. He drew his sword quickly and issued a challenge: "Art thou for us, or for our adversaries?" (Josh. 5:13).

The stranger answered calmly, "Nay; but as captain of the host of the Lord am I now come" (Josh. 5:14).

Realizing immediately that he was in the presence of a heavenly being, Joshua fell on his face before the man and asked, "What saith my lord unto his servant?"

The captain of the Lord's host replied, "Loose thy shoe from off thy foot; for the place whereon thou standest is holy" (Josh. 5:15).

The same command had been given to Moses as he came into God's presence at the burning bush, and Joshua instantly complied. We know that he was indeed talking with God, for Joshua 6:2 tells us, "And the Lord said unto Joshua, See, I have given unto thine hand Jericho, and the king thereof, and mighty men of valor."

Joshua was given explicit instructions. All of the Israelite men of war were to march around the city once each day for six days. On the seventh day they were to circle the walls seven times. Then, a long blast should be blown on the trumpets and all of the people were to shout loudly at once. Then, the Lord told Joshua, the walls would fall down flat and each man should run straight ahead into the city through the rubble of the collapsed walls.

All of the inhabitants were to be killed except Rahab, the harlot who had hidden the spies, and her family. There was to be no booty taken from this city. Only the silver and gold were to be preserved, and these were to be placed in the treasury of the Lord.

Joshua returned to Gilgal and called the people together. He related what the Lord had commanded them. The next morning the priests carried the ark of the covenant before the men of war, and they marched in silence around the walls of Jericho as the bewildered soldiers on the battlements watched in amazement. For six consecutive days they did the same thing, each time withdrawing to their camp in total silence without attacking the city.

But on the seventh day they circled the walls seven times. Just as they completed this Joshua gave a signal and the priests sounded a long blast with their ram's horn trumpets. The men responded with a tumultuous shout. Suddenly the stones of the foundations of the wall began to move. The undulating wave rose, reaching the very top of the wall. With a roar the mud-brick upper walls began to fall, and the entire structure fell down flat.

The Israelite soldiers charged, each man entering the city straight ahead from his position around the now collapsed wall: "And they utterly destroyed all that was in the city, both man and woman, young and old, and ox, and sheep, and ass, with the edge of the sword" (Josh. 6:21).

Did the Biblical Account Actually Happen?

The mound which now covers the ancient city of Jericho is called Tel es-Sultan and is close by the modern Arab town of Jericho. The site has been excavated several times, most recently by the British archaeologist Kathleen Kenyon. Although she died over a decade before her findings and conclusions were published, she had stated that in her opinion there was *no* city at this site at the time Joshua supposedly conquered it.

Are we to believe Kathleen Kenyon — or the Bible? Is the biblical account a fabricated story? Does our Bible contain an outright *lie*? Let's look at the history of the archaeological findings and determine the truth about Jericho's famous walls, and whether they did, indeed, "come tumblin' down" as the Israelites marched around them, blowing ram's horn trumpets and letting out a mighty shout.

Jericho was the second site in the Holy Land to be investigated, the first being Jerusalem itself. In 1868 the British engineer, Charles Warren, dug a series of six vertical shafts and three trenches. Warren[1] reported his findings with the conclusion that the mound called Tell es-Sultan was indeed artificial and contained man-made structures which he termed "castles." These were not really "ancient castles," but the remains of the fortifications and walls of the city of Jericho

The first major excavation was carried out by Ernst Sellin and Carl Watzinger in 1907.[2] Using the very inaccurate dating methods of the time, Watzinger stated that the fortifications were from the Late Bronze period (c. 1550-1200 B.C.), and concluded incorrectly that Jericho had been unoccupied when Joshua and the Israelites were purported to have taken the city.

The British archaeologist John Garstang excavated at Jericho from 1930 to 1936 and published a final report on his findings and conclusions in collaboration with his son.[3] Garstang unearthed a double city wall that had collapsed and found that the buildings that it had enclosed had been destroyed by fire. Based on pottery recovered from the debris, he concluded that this city had been razed in the time period of the Israelite invasion of Canaan. The evidence he uncovered indicated the method of destruction coincided exactly with the biblical account of Joshua.

Garstang wrote, "In a word, in all material details and in date, the fall of Jericho took place as described in the biblical narrative. Our demonstration is limited, however, to material observations: the walls fell, shaken apparently by an earthquake, and the city was destroyed by fire, about 1400 B.C. These are the basic facts resulting from our investigations. The link with Joshua and the Israelites is only circumstantial, but it seems to be solid and without a flaw."[4]

Garstang's conclusions started a heated debate among his colleagues. A young British archaeologist, Kathleen Kenyon, reviewed his findings and disputed his dating of the walls and the destroyed city. She placed them in the same time period that Sellin and Watzinger had previously placed them. Kathleen Kenyon led another excavation of the mound beginning in 1952 and continuing to 1958. She died in 1978 without publishing her final data, but based on preliminary published reports[5], her conclusion was that Jericho could not have been destroyed according to biblical accounts. These reports did not, however, contain detailed evidence, and it was not until 1982 and 1983, when two volumes were published on the pottery excavated in her field work, that other scholars could examine her work. Bryant D. Wood did just that, and in an excellent article published in the March/April 1990 issue of *Biblical Archaeology Review*, he gives the results of his analysis of Kathleen Kenyon's data, and his conclusions based on her findings.

Dr. Wood was intimately familiar with Garstang's field work and was intrigued by Garstang's report of a considerable quantity of Late Bronze Age pottery he had unearthed. This was what Kathleen Kenyon had repeatedly stated to be *absent* at Tell es-Sultan — the biblical Jericho. Kenyon had based her conclusion on what was *not* found at the site, rather than what was found at the site. It was also obvious that both Kenyon and Garstang had excavated in what would have been the very poor quarter of the city — containing only the humble, domestic dwellings.

In fact, Kenyon had written, "The picture given . . . is that of simple villagers. There is no suggestion at all of luxury . . . . It was quite probable that Jericho at this time was something of a backwater, away from the contacts with richer areas provided by the coastal route."[6]

Wood asked the following: "Why then would anyone expect to find exotic imported ceramics in this type of cultural milieu?" He further points out that Kenyon's conclusions are based on a very limited area of excavation, two 26 X 26 foot squares. Kenyon had theorized that Jericho had been razed by the Egyptians, or the Hyksos fleeing from the Egyptians. This, he points out, can be argued against by Kenyon's own data. She had found jars full of grain in parts of the city which had been ravaged by fire.

The Egyptians took cities by siege, not by direct assault. Hence, there would not have been full jars of grain left after the city had been starved into submission by the Egyptians. On the other hand, why would the Hyksos have *destroyed* the very cities *to which they had been fleeing for safety?* Jericho, obviously, had not been destroyed by either the Egyptians nor the Hyksos.

Then whose army was responsible for the crumbled walls and the fire-gutted buildings which were very much in evidence at ancient Jericho?

As Bryant Wood carefully examined Kenyon's own data, he found that her own evidence, far from disputing Garstang's conclusion that the biblical account was correct, *actually supports* that conclusion. The pottery Kenyon found is obviously Late Bronze Age I. She had apparently also ignored some of Garstang's most important data, the finding of pottery decorated with red and black paint which appears to be *imported* Cypriot bichrome, the very type of pottery she looked for but did not find — and the absence of which she had based much of her conclusion on. From this, one is led to wonder whether Kenyon was not aware of Garstang's finds, or simply ignored them.

Dr. Wood is convinced that Garstang was correct, and this is based on other evidence as well as the pottery. Stratigraphic considerations of the debris of the walls, scarabs found in those digs, full jars of grain which point to an attack *after* an abundant spring harvest, and a radio-carbon dating of a charcoal sample taken from the debris which indicates that the city was destroyed in 1401 B.C., plus or minus 40 years[7], all support Garstang.

Bryant Wood's examination of *all* of the accumulated data concerning the dating of the ruins of ancient Jericho should finally silence those scholars who dispute the biblical account — but it probably won't. The argument will still go on despite the overwhelming evidence that Dr. Wood presents.

But what about the walls? Did they really fall down as the Bible tells us they did? Let us look at the archaeological evidence and try to find the proof for this.

The Walls of Jericho

From the excavated mound of the ancient city of Jericho, the shovels have unearthed the very stones which comprised the walls surrounding it in Joshua's time. It is possible to get an accurate picture of them from the debris and from the sections which still stand. It was indeed an imposing and intimidating fortress.

The outer defense was a stone revetment wall rising fifteen feet above the plain. This held in place a high rampart, topped by a parapet wall of mud-brick construction. The house walls were only one brick in thickness.

It was in one of these houses that Rahab, the harlot, lived and it was from a window of this house that she let down Joshua's spies on a flaxen rope.

The city of Jericho was of an elongated oval shape, about a thousand feet in length and five hundred feet in width. The outer wall would have been about a half mile in circumference. Within the walls was a spring which supplied the city's water and which now fills a reservoir for the modern Arab town of Jericho.

It would have presented a most formidable obstacle for any invading army. It was well stocked with food, had an ample source of water, and it would have been able to withstand a direct assault, or a prolonged siege.

Within the excavated ruins has been found a huge, round, stone building still standing today which was probably the grain silo. This may be the oldest man-made structure ever found anywhere.

The Israelites would certainly have had a difficult time if they had been forced to capture this almost impregnable fortress by conventional means when they entered Canaan. But the Bible tells us that God made it easy for them.

What Happened to These Walls?

In Bryant G. Wood's article in *Biblical Archaeology Review,* he sums up the evidence which Kenyon and others have found which substantiates the biblical account of what happened to the walls of Jericho.

He states, "Despite the fact that the area where the upper wall once stood is gone, there is evidence, incredible as it may seem, that this wall came tumbling down and, in the words of the biblical account in Joshua, 'fell down flat' " (Josh. 6:20). Again, the evidence comes from Kenyon's own careful stratigraphic excavation and the detailed, final report that describes it.

What Kathleen Kenyon's report shows is that the upper wall, made of red mud-bricks on top of the revetment wall, came tumbling down and fell over the outer revetment wall. They lie there today in a heap. To quote Kenyon, "The destruction was complete. Walls and floors were blackened or reddened by fire, and every room was filled with fallen bricks, timbers, and household utensils; in most rooms the fallen debris was heavily burnt, but the collapse of the walls of the eastern rooms seems to have taken place before they were affected by the fire."[8]

Wood says, "The last observation in this quotation suggests that an earthquake preceded the conflagration. This description may be compared with the biblical account. According to the Bible, after the Israelites gained access to the city, they 'burned the city with fire and all that was therein' (Josh. 6:24). In short, after the collapse of the walls — perhaps by earthquake — the city was put to the torch."[9]

The manner in which the walls collapsed, Wood also points out, agrees with the biblical account which states that the Israelites "went up into the city, every man straight before him" (Josh. 6:20). He notes that the account specifically tells us that they went *up* into the city. The collapsed upper walls would have fallen down on top of the fallen outer revetment walls, making a very convenient ramp for the Israelites to have charged *up* and *over* the debris to enter Jericho.

The walls of this city indeed seem to have "come tumbling down," just as the Bible tells us that they did. And as additional archaeological evidence comes in, the biblical account of what happened gains in credibility. Dr. Wood lists the already accumulated evidence which substantiates the accuracy of the biblical account of the conquest of Jericho by Joshua's army.[10]

• The city was strongly fortified (Josh. 2:5,7,15; 6:5,20).
• The attack occurred just after harvest time in the spring of the year (Josh. 2:6; 3:15; 5:10).
• The occupants of the city had no opportunity to flee with their foodstuffs (Josh. 6:1).
• The siege was short (Josh. 6:15).
• The walls were leveled, possibly by an earthquake (Josh. 6:20).
• The city was not plundered (Josh. 6:17-18).
• The city was burned (Josh. 6:24).

Dr. Wood admits that much controversy remains regarding the date of the Israelite conquest of Canaan, but as new data comes to light and the old data is re-evaluated, there is increasing evidence that the Israelites actually *were* in Canaan in a time which agrees with the dating of the destruction of the city of Jericho in about 1400 B.C.

Since the date presented indicates that it was neither the Egyptians nor the Hyksos who were responsible for the destruction of ancient Jericho, that really leaves *only* the Israelites under the command of Joshua, as God's Word plainly states, who were responsible.

What Made the Walls Fall?

We have examined the evidence that the walls of Jericho did indeed collapse, and exactly as the Bible tells us that they did. Archaeology confirms that the city was not looted; that the attack came in the spring just after harvest time; that it took a short time for the invaders to conquer it; and that there was no opportunity for the residents to flee. But what actually caused these walls to fall? Is there any evidence which might answer this question?

Yes, there is. There is ample evidence that the walls were felled by an earthquake. Geophysicist Amos Nur writes, "This combination, the destruction of Jericho and the stoppage of the Jordan, is so typical of earthquakes in this region that only little doubt can be left as to the reality of such events in Joshua's time."[11]

The two events, the crossing of the Jordan River after the flow of water stopped, and the destruction of the walls of Jericho, are closely related — both in time and in cause. It is probable that the earth tremor which dammed the Jordan was a foreshock of the larger earthquake which demolished the walls of Jericho.

God, in His precise timing, had ordained that these two movements of the earth occur at *exactly* the right time to first allow the Israelites to cross a swollen river on dry land, then to capture a heavily fortified city in a miraculous way. Again, His complete and total control of *His* creation has been demonstrated by miracles.

A Bitter Postscript to the Battle of Jericho

God had commanded that the Israelites take nothing from Jericho except for the gold, silver, and vessels of brass and iron which were to be placed in the treasury of the Lord (Josh. 6:24). This order had been obeyed by all but *one* of Joshua's soldiers. For this one man's transgression, *all* of the Israelites would have to be punished.

After Jericho, the next city to be assaulted was Ai, located over the hills about twelve miles to the east. Joshua sent men out to survey Ai's defenses and they returned with a very favorable report. "And they returned to Joshua, and said unto him, Let not all the people go up; but let about two or three thousand men go up and smite Ai; and make not all the people to labour thither; for they are but few" (Josh. 7:3).

The soldiers were extremely confident after the miraculous victory at Jericho. The defenders of Ai were few in number, and they were certain that they could take this city with but a small force of men. So Joshua sent only about three thousand men to capture Ai. The result, however was not what they had anticipated. "And the men of Ai smote of them about thirty and six men: for they chased them from before the gate even unto Shebarim, and smote them in the going down: wherefore the hearts of the people melted, and became as water" (Josh. 7:5).

They had been defeated! How could this happen? Had not God promised that He would go before them and defeat their enemies? What had happened?

Joshua and the elders of Israel tore their clothes and fell to their faces before the Lord, asking why this had occurred. God answered. He informed them that Israel had sinned, taking of the accursed possessions of the inhabitants of Jericho and hiding them among their own things. God had allowed this defeat, and the punishment of all of the Israelites to occur, because this *one* man had not obeyed the commandment of the Lord.

Joshua assembled all the tribes of Israel, and under the guidance of the Lord, he pointed out the tribe of Judah. Out of Judah he singled out the family of the Zarhites, and from that family, man by man, he came to Zabdi. From Zabdi's household was found the one man who was responsible for Israel's sin — Achan.

When confronted, Achan confessed. "And Achan answered Joshua and said, Indeed I have sinned against the Lord God of Israel, and thus have I done: When I saw among the spoils a goodly Babylonian garment, and two hundred shekels of silver, and a wedge of gold of fifty shekels weight, then I coveted them, and took them; and behold, they are hid in the earth in the midst of my tent, and the silver is under it" (Josh. 7:20-21).

Joshua's men found the hidden booty which Achan had taken from Jericho. They brought it and his sons and daughters, his cattle and his tent, and all of his possessions to the valley which is now called Achor. He was stoned to death and all he had was burned and covered with a heap of stones.

Then the Lord's anger was turned away, and God restored His promises to Israel. The city of Ai was then taken easily, and the spoils of Ai were shared by all the people.

The lesson here is, I believe, that those who call upon the Lord for protection and to supply all their needs must make absolutely sure to walk totally in His will and observe *all* that He has commanded us.

Achan tried to cheat God. No one gets away with that!

15

Did the Sun Really Move Backward?

Over the years I have met a number of people who have told me that they could not believe the Bible because there are some things in it which are *absolutely impossible* to have happened. When asked what these things are, most refer to the incident in 2 Kings 20 where they say the Bible states that God made the sun move backward. This, they say, is utter nonsense, that the sun *could not have moved backward,* for this would have meant that the earth would have reversed its direction of spin.

I readily agree with these people. The sun cannot move backward. The earth did *not* reverse its spin.

But then I hasten to tell them this is not what the Bible says at all. That's what they have heard someone *say* that the Bible says.

Let's see for ourselves what we are told, and investigate whether this can be explained by science in a manner acceptable to skeptical minds and still preserve what we may call a "miracle" from the hand of God.

In 2 Kings 20 we are told that King Hezekiah became seriously ill. Isaiah, the prophet, came to the king with bad news. He told Hezekiah, "Set thine house in order; for thou shalt die and not live." This was not just Isaiah's opinion, for he had prefaced his statement with, "Thus saith the Lord." Hezekiah knew that his time was up.

Hezekiah had been a good king. He had been a righteous man before the Lord. Ahaz, his father, had been an evil man. He had turned Israel into an idolatrous nation, worshipping false gods. Ahaz had even offered his son through the fire to the Canaanite god, Baal. But when Ahaz died and the twenty-five year old Hezekiah became king of Israel, he quickly turned things around. He removed the pagan idols, altars, and sacred groves. He even smashed to pieces the brazen serpent that Moses had made, for the Israelites had made that into an idol and had worshipped it.

The temple had fallen into disrepair, and Hezekiah had cleansed it and restored the worship of the Lord in the temple that Solomon had built. And the Lord had blessed Hezekiah and had protected Judah from the ravages of the king of Assyria even when his army had been at the gates of Jerusalem. But Hezekiah knew that after he was dead, his sons would not fear the Lord and his land would be laid desolate. Hezekiah turned his face to the wall and prayed to the Lord, "I beseech thee, O Lord, remember now how I have walked before thee in truth and with a perfect heart, and have done that which is good in thy sight. And Hezekiah wept sore" (2 Kings 20:3).

Before Isaiah had even left the king's court, the word of the Lord came to him again. He returned to Hezekiah with a different message. "Thus saith the Lord, the God of David, thy father, I have heard thy prayer, I have seen thy tears: behold, I will heal thee: on the third day thou shalt go up unto the house of the Lord. And I will add unto thy days fifteen years . . ." (2 Kings 20:5-6).

Isaiah took a lump of figs and laid it upon Hezekiah's terrible boil and Hezekiah's boil was healed. But still Hezekiah was not totally convinced that the Lord would restore him to health. He asked for a sign from God. "And Hezekiah said unto Isaiah, What shall be the sign that the Lord will heal me, and that I shall go up into the house of the Lord the third day? And Isaiah said, This sign shalt thou have of the Lord, that the Lord will do the thing that he hath spoken: shall the shadow go forward ten degrees, or go back ten degrees?" (2 Kings 20:8-9).

Hezekiah had the choice. Would he want the Lord to make the shadow on the sundial go backward or forward? The Lord would do either one, as Hezekiah chose. "And Hezekiah answered, it is a light thing for the shadow to go down ten degrees: nay, but let the shadow return backward ten degrees" (2 Kings 20:10).

Please note that nothing is said in the Bible about the *sun* actually moving. The shadow on the sundial would do the moving — not the sun itself. We know that the sun does not move anyway. It is the rotation of the earth that causes the sun to *seem* to come up in the east and set in the west. So Isaiah cried out to the Lord which way Hezekiah had chosen. "... and he brought the shadow ten degrees backward, by which it had gone down in the dial of Ahaz" (2 Kings 20:11). The sun did not move. The earth had not reversed its rotation. Only the *shadow* on the sundial in the courtyard moved. This is an excellent case in point where many people *think* the Bible has said something when it has not said that, at all. I just wonder how many Christians, who have been in Sunday school since children, are surprised at what the Bible actually says in this case.

How Did God Make the Shadow Move Backward?

The position of the shadow of the pole on a sundial is caused by the angle of the sun's position relative to the location of the sundial on earth. Since the earth revolves around the sun, it is readily apparent that the sun cannot move. The length of a day is determined by the rotation of the earth on its axis, the inclination of the earth, and the time of year, with days being longer in summer and shorter in winter in the northern hemisphere, and just the opposite in the southern hemisphere.

Then whatever happened to make the shadow on Hezekiah's sundial move backward had to do with conditions on the earth itself. Did the earth suddenly reverse its direction of rotation? Hardly, for this would have triggered catastrophic events on the earth. Did the earth's inclination change? No, this would have meant a change in seasons and a sudden alteration of the earth's climate.

What, then, did cause the shadow on this particular sundial to move backward by ten degrees? The answer is surprisingly simple. To understand what did happen, we must first examine a few facts concerning the light from the sun as it passes through the vacuum of space and enters the earth's atmosphere.

Light travels at its maximum speed through empty space, what we call a vacuum. The speed of light through this emptiness can be measured at approximately 186,000 miles per second. But when light leaves a vacuum and must pass through a medium which has a density, which is to say it has a mass, the speed of light is reduced. And when the speed of light is reduced, its direction is altered.

If we look into a pond or stream and see a fish in the water, where that fish appears to be is not where it actually is. The light waves carrying the image of that fish have been altered in direction by passing through the water. The angle at which we are looking into the water determines how close the image of the fish is to the fish's actual position. It is only when we are directly over the fish and look down at a 90° angle that we see the fish where it really is in the water. The angle of incidence, how far from directly over the fish we are, determines the angle of refraction — where the fish *appears* to be.

It may surprise many readers to know that the sun is not really where we see it in the sky, unless it is exactly overhead. It is really at a *lower* point relative to the horizon. In fact, we "see" the sunrise before the sun should be visible because the earth's atmosphere bends the sunlight at an angle which allows us to see it before it comes over the horizon. Conversely, we are able to see the sun *after* it has set behind the horizon at sunset for the same reason.

Any substance through which light can pass has what is called an index of refraction, which is the ratio of the speed of light in a vacuum divided by the speed of light through that substance. The higher the index of refraction, the greater the angle that light is bent away from what would be its normal path.

The diagram below illustrates how an observer on earth sees the sun through the earth's atmosphere, which bends the light rays.

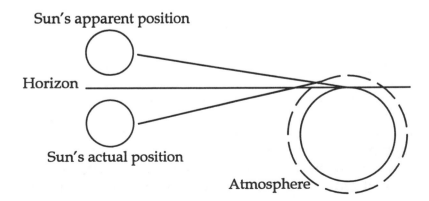

Sun's apparent position

Horizon

Sun's actual position

Atmosphere

As you can see from this diagram, an observer would see the sun before it was above the horizon due to the bending of the light rays from the sun by the optical density of the earth's atmosphere. Any shadow cast by an object on earth, therefore, does not reflect the *actual* position of the sun, but the *degree of distortion or bending* of the sun's rays by the optical density of the earth's atmosphere. If that optical density were to change, the angle of refraction would also change. So would the position of a shadow on a sundial. And this is exactly what could have taken place when Hezekiah watched the shadow on the sundial in the courtyard of his house in Jerusalem.

It would not have been necessary for the optical density of a large portion of the atmosphere to have changed, but only that part which was between the sundial Hezekiah was watching and the point at which the sun's rays entered the atmosphere. In fact, it could have been quite localized. A cloud containing a large amount of finely divided material would have sufficed. A high altitude accumulation of water vapor could have accomplished this. Anything which would have increased the optical density of the normal air between Hezekiah's sundial and the point at which the sun's rays entered the earth's atmosphere would have caused this phenomenon to have happened.

Was There a Miracle Here?

Yes, I would certainly call this a miracle from God, although all Hezekiah asked for was a simple sign. He was given a choice by God, either to have the shadow move forward or backward by ten degrees. It was Hezekiah's choice. God was, therefore, prepared to alter the optical density of the air to accomplish either one. We can define a miracle as God's direct intervention in what would be considered the *only* normal outcome of an event. In this case He again used a natural principle of physics to accomplish the unexpected and unusual. Normally a shadow on a sundial does not move backward. On Hezekiah's sundial it did. This was certainly God's intervention in what would normally have occurred. According to our definition it is without question a miracle. Does this in any way diminish our respect for God's power? No, not at all. God created this universe and He ordained the laws of nature, including those of physics. If He chose to use one of His own natural laws of science to accomplish this, who are we to argue with the Creator? God can do anything He chooses to do.

Again, let me restate what I said at the beginning of this chapter about being absolutely certain of what the Bible says and does not say. If you are certain in your own mind just what God promised to do, and what He actually did, and you can understand the principle He used to accomplish it, then you can be prepared to not only withstand the challenge of a skeptical and unbelieving world, but also effectively answer this skepticism with facts. You and I were called to be witnesses in this world. Let's do our homework and be proficient witnesses to the truth of His Word.

But to finish Hezekiah's story, he did live for another fifteen years, just as God had said he would. He was succeeded by his son, Manasseh, who turned out, as Hezekiah had expected, to be an evil man. Manasseh restored all of the heathen altars and high places that his father had torn down and turned the temple into a pagan shrine of worship. His sons also did that which was evil in the sight of God, and eventually God punished the people of Judah. God raised up the Babylonian empire and a king named Nebuchadnezzar. You know the rest of the story.

16

What Really Happened to Sodom and Gomorrah?

About four thousand years ago, something very spectacular happened near the southern end of the Dead Sea.

In Genesis chapters 18 and 19 we are told of the destruction of the cities of Sodom and Gomorrah, along with several other corrupt cities of the plain near the lower part of the Dead Sea. This account begins with the Lord's visit with Abraham at Mamre which was located close to the modern Arab town of Hebron. When Abraham and his nephew, Lot, had returned from Egypt with great herds, the land could not sustain both of them and they had to part company. Lot had decided to take his herds toward the plains of Jordan, while Abraham's cattle would graze in the land of central Canaan.

The landscape of these areas is quite different today from what Genesis tells us it was at that time. "And Lot lifted up his eyes, and beheld all the plain of Jordan, that it was well watered every where, before the Lord destroyed Sodom and Gomorrah, even as the garden of the Lord, like the land of Egypt, as thou comest unto Zoar" (Gen. 13:10).

Today the area around the Dead Sea which Lot had chosen is for the most part desolate and barren. Something *must* have happened to this entire area for the radical difference we see in it at the present time.

The Lord informed Abraham that He intended to destroy the cities of Sodom and Gomorrah, whose sin He could no longer tolerate. That evening two angels entered Sodom, where they encountered Lot sitting at the gate. The men of the city also saw these handsome strangers and tried to force their way into Lot's house to sodomize them. The sin of homosexuality was the major reason God had chosen to destroy these cities.

The angels struck their attackers blind and warned Lot and his family to leave Sodom before dawn the next day and to flee into the mountains. Lot received permission to go to the town of Zoar. Early in the morning Lot, his wife, and his two daughters fled from Sodom. "Then the Lord rained upon Sodom and upon Gomorrah brimstone and fire from the Lord out of heaven; And he overthrew those cities, and all the plain, and all the inhabitants of the cities, and that which grew upon the ground" (Gen. 19:24–25).

Abraham could see that something catastrophic was happening as he watched from thirty miles away. Genesis 19:28 tells us, "And he looked toward Sodom and Gomorrah, and toward all the land of the plain, and beheld, and, lo, the smoke of the country went up as the smoke of a furnace."

The angels had warned Lot's family not to look back, but Lot's wife could not resist. "But his wife looked back from behind him, and she became a pillar of salt" (Gen. 19:26).

Could This Actually Have Happened?

There has been a dispute among many biblical scholars about whether this story of the destruction of Sodom and Gomorrah can be taken *literally*, or is only an allegorical representation to warn against the type of sin that the Lord called an abomination to Him. The cities named are certainly no longer in existence, and no record other than in the Bible could be found that they ever did. Is the Genesis account an actual event or an outright fabrication?

There is much at stake in the answer to this question, for if the Genesis story of the destruction of Sodom and Gomorrah is totally untrue, then *other* events the Bible tells us of could also be fiction. The credibility of the *entire* Old Testament could be in jeopardy.

If no one could prove where Sodom and Gomorrah had been located, or even whether they had actually existed, it would be almost impossible to authenticate the Genesis account of what happened to them. But then archaeologists made an extraordinary find.

Sodom and Gomorrah Located

The proof came from an unexpected source. In 1964, archaeologists began to dig in northern Syria at a site named Tell Mardikh. What they found was the ancient city of Ebla, once the capital of a vast empire. A team of Italians unearthed the royal library containing thousands of clay tablets, written in cuneiform, in a Semite language very similar to Hebrew.[1]

These were records dating back as far as 2300 B.C. When the translations of these clay tablets began to be published, they provided some astonishing information. In the list of the kings of Ebla was a man by the name of Eber.[2] A man of the same name is mentioned in Genesis 10:24-25 and 11:14-17, who begat a son named Peleg.

The royal library of Ebla also contained a geographical atlas. This listed the principal cities trading with Ebla's merchants. In this list we find the names of both Sodom and Gomorrah, and the other cities of the plain which Genesis tells us were destroyed by the Lord in the time of Abraham.

The exact location of the ancient cities of Sodom and Gomorrah were confirmed when a Byzantine mosaic map was unearthed which gave the location of Zoar, the city to which Lot fled, at the southern end of the Dead Sea. As it took Lot and his daughters only a few hours to reach safety in a cave near this town, Sodom must have been in the same general area.

If we examine the chronology, we find that Eber, named as a major king of the empire of Ebla, was born in about 2451 B.C. He lived for 464 years, dying in about 1987 B.C. Abraham was born in about 2166 B.C. and lived for 175 years, dying in about 1991 B.C. Although Abraham was a descendent of Eber through Terah, Nahor, Serug, Reu, and Peleg, they were also alive at the same time at the end of Eber's life.

It is very probably that it is from Eber that the name *Hebrew* originated. In fact, Josephus tells us in *Antiquities of the Jews*, "Sala was the son of Arphaxad; and his son was Heber, from whom they originally called the Jews, Hebrews."[3] This certainly makes sense, for we are told in Genesis 14:13, "And there came one that had escaped, and told Abram the Hebrew . . . ." It stands to reason that if Abraham was a descendent of Eber he would have borne the same ethnic appellative as the man whose name had originated it.

The clay tablets found at Ebla also mention the city of Salem, where in Genesis 14:18 Melchizedek, king of Salem, blesses Abraham. Salem means "peace" and the city's name eventually became Jeru-Salem, or "New Peace."

The Ugarit Tablets, found in what is today Lebanon, contain hundreds of Hebrew words and dozens of phrases which are also found in the Old Testament,[4] giving testimony to the wide use of this language in ancient times.

The science of archaeology has confirmed that the cities of Sodom and Gomorrah actually existed at the southern end of the Dead Sea, but what happened to those cities? Can science throw any light on what caused their destruction?

The Destruction of Sodom and Gomorrah

In order to understand what caused the cataclysmic destruction of Sodom and Gomorrah, it is necessary to first understand the geology of that region. These cities once stood at the southeastern end of where the Dead Sea was *at that time*, before about 1900 B.C. when the disaster occurred.

The Dead Sea is located in the most unique geological area in the world, along the Great Rift, a long and active fault line which begins in Turkey, cuts through the Middle East and the Red Sea, and ends in Africa. It resembles a "slice" taken out of the planet, seismically active and smouldering with volcanic potential.

The Dead Sea, which has no outlet, is the lowest point on earth at 1,292 feet below sea level. It is 1,200 feet deep in places, and at the bottom is a full half-mile below sea level. Because it has no outlet it accumulates salt and other minerals, making it the richest source of these minerals in the world.

From the bottom of the Dead Sea petroleum exudes, and there is a smell of oil and sulphur. Along its banks gathers the heavier residues of asphalt, the "slime" which is mentioned in Genesis 14:10.

The cities of Sodom and Gomorrah were located in what the Bible calls "the Vale of Siddim." This can be located today, immediately south of the tongue of land which juts out from the Jordanian side of the sea, northwest of Al Karak.

To the north of this peninsula the water drops off sharply to a depth of 1,200 feet, but to the south lies a shallow bay only about 50 feet in depth. This bay to the south was where the cities of Sodom and Gomorrah once stood. Beneath the water of this bay can be seen the salt-encrusted outlines of forests, and it is beneath this water that the ruins of Sodom and Gomorrah rest.

The Phoenician priest Sanchuniathon wrote in his redis-covered book, *Ancient History,* "The Vale of Sidimus sank and became a lake, always evaporating and containing no fish, a symbol of vengeance and of death for the transgressor."[5]

The Genesis account of the destruction of these cities gives us a picture of a *typical* seismic event, accompanied by a fissure which erupted with molten rock and sulphurous gasses. Bolts of lightning would have streaked from the billowing clouds of volcanic debris, also typical of such an event. Then, after these cities in the Vale of Siddim had been devastated by thousands of tons of rock and volcanic debris, the area sank fifty feet and was swallowed by the waters of the Dead Sea.

Three nearby towns have been excavated and archaeolo-gists have found a layer of volcanic ash covering them. There is absolutely no doubt that the Genesis account, recorded by Abraham, is correct in every detail. The Lord destroyed these cities by volcanic activity, followed by an earthquake which opened the earth and devoured all traces of them beneath the caustic brine of the Dead Sea.

The land around this area today is barren and almost devoid of life. Only in the occasional oasis where small springs bubble fresh water to the surface can vegetation grow. The volcanic event spewed salt and harsh minerals over the fertile plain, condemning it to perpetual sterility.

And what about Lot's wife who was turned to a pillar of salt? Not far from where the ancient city of Zoar once stood, there is a pinnacle of salt which resembles somewhat the figure of a woman. As long as anyone can remember, the Bedouins who occasionally pass this way have referred to it as "Lot's Wife."

17

Did the Whale Really Swallow Jonah?

On first reading, the Book of Jonah sounds preposterous to many people. This short book appears in the Old Testament among those written by authentic Hebrew prophets, telling an incredible story of a man who was swallowed by a big fish, spent three days inside that fish, and lived.

Another seeming discrepancy is the statement made that he was commanded by God to go to Nineveh from his home near Nazareth to preach their impending destruction, and that this was ". . . an exceeding great city of three day's journey" (Jon. 3:3). The distance from Nazareth to Nineveh is over five hundred miles. How could this be a journey of only three days?

This story about Jonah is a stumbling block to unbelievers who say that if they are expected to accept this sort of obvious fiction, then they certainly cannot have any confidence in *anything* the Bible tells us.

Is this story of Jonah only a parable — or a myth — which only serves to strike home a point? Or did it actually happen just as the Bible states that it did? Is there any scientific evidence that this seemingly impossible event *actually could have taken place?*

Let us examine the circumstances and see for ourselves.

Jonah's Call from the Lord

Jonah, which means "dove," was the son of Amitti and lived in Gath-hepher, about three miles from Nazareth in Galilee during the early part of the reign of Jeroboam II (782-753 B.C.). We are told that the Word of the Lord came to him to travel to the city of Nineveh, and to preach to the inhabitants of their wickedness and coming destruction.

Now Nineveh was the capital of Assyria, and the Assyrians were a fierce people. For a Jew to go there and denounce them in that fashion would very probably mean torture and a slow and painful death. Jonah, to put it mildly, was terrified.

Jonah traveled all right, but he went in the opposite direction. He went to the seaport of Joppa and took a ship bound for Tarshish — about as far away from Nineveh as he could go. But God would not let him escape. He sent a great wind and the ship was caught in a mighty storm. As they were about to sink, the sailors looked for the cause of their trouble, and Jonah was found to be the source of their problem for disobeying God.

Jonah was thrown overboard. "Now the Lord had prepared a great fish to swallow up Jonah. And Jonah was in the belly of the fish three days and three nights" (Jon. 1:17).

Inside the fish Jonah repented and prayed, promising to do what the Lord had commanded him to do. "And the Lord spake unto the fish, and it vomited out Jonah upon the dry land" (Jon. 2:10).

Jonah Preaches to Nineveh

With the wrath and power of the Lord fresh in his mind, Jonah went to Nineveh — probably realizing that no matter what fate awaited him at the hands of the Assyrians, it would not compare with what God would do to him if he did not go. "And Jonah began to enter into the city a day's journey, and he cried, and said, Yet forty days, and Nineveh shall be overthrown" (Jon. 3:4).

Much to his surprise, the people took him seriously. They proclaimed a fast, put on sackcloth, and repented of their sins. Even the king did this. As a result, God changed His mind about destroying the city.

The Angry Prophet

Instead of being elated that the Assyrians had repented, and much relieved that they had not killed him, Jonah got mad. After all, Jonah fumed, he had come this far to preach the destruction of Nineveh, and the hated, pagan Assyrians who lived there! Now God wasn't going to destroy them after all! It was not fair! God had let him down!

Jonah sulked. He went to the outskirts of the city and sat down on the ground, angry at God. It was hot, and the sun beat unmercifully upon him. He wanted to die. He had been made a fool of, and he certainly could not go back and face the people of Nazareth who would ridicule him for prophesying the cataclysm which had not occurred.

God, in His mercy, caused a gourd to grow up and shade the troubled man from the torrid sun, but Jonah continued to be angry with God. So the Lord sent a worm which cut the stem of the plant, leaving Jonah exposed again to bake in the scorching sun.

God Explains Why

In a few, brief verses God explains that He will have mercy, even on unbelievers, when they repent and turn from their wickedness. It is interesting to note that Jonah was the *first* Hebrew to be sent out of Israel to another nation as a missionary. Jesus, who also came from Nazareth, refers to him and states that the only sign the Jews would receive would be the sign of the prophet Jonah — the three days and three nights He would be in the tomb before His Resurrection.

Would Jesus have spoken in this manner of an incident that never happened? Let us see what evidence there is that this man named Jonah really lived, and that the things written about him actually occurred.

The Evidence

Did this man Jonah exist, or is the whole story a fabrication? If you travel from the town of Nazareth northeast toward Cana, you may find today a village called Meshhed where the traditional tomb of Jonah the prophet is located.[1] A mile away is the place where he was born, the village of Gath-hepher, or Khirbet ez-zurra. There can be very little doubt that a historical person named Jonah lived, and in the time frame necessary for the events related to be possible. Nineveh was eventually destroyed in 612 B.C., and the destruction was so complete that the city itself was considered a myth until it was unearthed by Sir Austen Layard in the nineteenth century.

In Jonah's time, Nineveh was one of the greatest cities on

earth. It was enclosed by walls almost eight miles in circumference, and its suburbs sprawled along the Tigris River for quite a distance. The ruins were marked by two large mounds, one called Quyunjiq and the other called Nebi Yunus — which means "Prophet Jonah." There can be little doubt that a man named Jonah had something very special to do with this ancient city of Nineveh.

One of the difficulties encountered with the credibility of the Book of Jonah may be easily resolved by noting the gigantic size of this city. Jonah seems to tell us that it was only three day's journey from his home near Nazareth to Nineveh. But that's not what he meant, at all. What he was telling us was that it would take three days *to walk around* this huge metropolis. This is clear from Jonah 3:4 where he began to preach after he had entered the city and had walked for a full day without reaching the center of it.

But what about being swallowed by the whale? Was this possible?

Can Anyone Be Swallowed by a Whale — and Survive?

Although the Book of Jonah tells us it was a "great fish," Jesus clarified this when He stated that Jonah spent three days and three nights in the belly of a *whale* (Matt. 12:40). The Greek word which Jesus used does not mean fish, it means a whale — although it is sometimes translated as "sea monster."

Few whales now inhabit the Mediterranean Sea where the incident must have taken place, but there is one species, the sperm whale, which is sometimes found there. This sea mammal is physically capable of swallowing a human being. A large whale can have a mouth as much as twelve feet wide, more than adequate for a man's body to enter. In addition, an enlargement of the whale's nasal sinus provides sufficient storage of air to make it theoretically possible for a man to *breathe* for several days.[2]

But have there been any actual confirmed reports that this has occurred? Yes, there have!

There are documented cases where sailors have survived after being ingested, vomited up, and rescued *alive*.[3] These are rare — very rare, indeed — but it can happen and it has!

The type of whale which swallowed Jonah was not a meat-eater. The digestive system of this whale could not reduce this "strange food" the whale had swallowed. Jonah actually made the whale sick — of indigestion. We know that when whales become sick they often beach themselves. After several days of nausea, Jonah's whale probably did the same thing.

And what does any animal — or human — do when it is sick to the stomach? It throws up! The whale vomited Jonah up on the sandy shore where it had beached itself.

The point remains whether or not *God* caused these events to happen. Did He really send the great wind which stirred up the waves and almost sank the boat on which Jonah was fleeing? Did the Lord prepare the great fish to swallow him after he had been thrown overboard? Did God speak to the whale which then vomited Jonah up on the dry land? I am convinced that God did do all of these things. Certainly the One who spoke the universe into existence, who created life itself, is capable of doing *anything* He wishes to do.

The evidence proves conclusively that *all* of the events described in the Book of Jonah are physically possible. But what is the reason that God did this?

The Lesson of the Book of Jonah

The Hebrews were a selfish, proud, and nationalistic people. They had been chosen by God as *His* very own nation. They were special — and they were reluctant to share this position with anyone else. But God had other plans.

The Lord declared His purpose for Israel in Isaiah 49:6: "I will also give thee for a light to the Gentiles, that thou mayest be my salvation unto the end of the earth." Jonah may have been the first Hebrew to be sent as an individual missionary to a Gentile nation, but God had declared His might and power to all countries which had come into contact with His chosen people, Israel.

In the plagues which finally convinced Pharaoh to let the Hebrews go free, God demonstrated His power to the Egyptians. When the walls of Jericho fell, the Canaanites were terrified, for the God of Israel went before them to fight. Nebuchadnezzar was stunned by the Lord's authority when Shadrach, Meshach, and Abednego emerged from the furnace unscathed.

God's plan was completed when His Son, Jesus, gave His life for the salvation of all men, Jew and Gentile alike. Paul was chosen to be the principal bearer of this gospel to the Gentile world, and unlike Jonah — the reluctant prophet — Paul went willingly.

The story of Jonah provides something else of great importance to us, for the three days and nights that he was "dead" in the belly of the great fish were to be used as a sign by Jesus Christ, who was to be in the earth — dead — for the same time until, like Jonah, He was resurrected to life.

The moral of the story of Jonah for us is that we should *not* resist God's calling. The belly of a whale can be a very uncomfortable place.

18

The Two Temples Destroyed — on Exactly the Same Day

In a previous chapter we became aware of how God is in complete control of even the very dates on which events happen in His world. We examined *seven* major events in the Bible which had occurred on exactly the same day of the Hebrew calendar — the seventeenth day of Nisan. In this chapter we will look at two identical events — the destruction of the first temple, built by Solomon, and the second temple, begun after the return from Babylonian captivity and completed by Herod.

We will find that both of these temples were destroyed on *exactly* the same day of the Hebrew calendar. I believe that this is yet another sign from the Almighty that He is indeed in control of time and the events in history.

The Houses of God

God doesn't *need* a structure built by man. Man, however, from time immemorial has needed a *place* where he could identify with worship. Pagan religions built great temples, and still do even today. Within them are found the man-made objects which are either worshipped directly or are symbols of the gods they represent. On the Acropolis in Athens the Greeks built magnificent temples to their pantheon of gods. The Parthenon has been called the most beautiful building man has ever built.

India has tens of thousands of temples, as do many other nations. In Christian countries we find towering cathedrals with lofty spires and ornate furnishings, magnificent altars, and stained glass windows. But it is not God who needs these resplendent edifices — it is man who needs them.

The Hebrews were no different. The patriarchs built altars of unhewn stones to offer sacrifices as they wandered with their herds, and these places were regularly visited by those seeking Yahweh's blessing. After the Exodus, as they traveled for forty years in the wilderness, the tabernacle was carried with them and pitched whenever they camped for any length of time. It was here that Moses spoke with the Lord, and sought His direction and will for Israel.

David offered to build a house for God, and finally the Lord accepted. But it would not be David who would build it, but Solomon, his son. It was not that God needed this house, but that the Hebrews needed it. When the first temple was completed after seven years of construction (1 Kings 6:38), it was the marvel of architecture of the time. And well it should have been, for it was God who gave the plans for all details of it.

Within the Holy of Holies was the ark of the covenant containing the stone tablets, written by the hand of God and given to Moses. Above the ark were the golden cherubims, whose wings covered the mercy seat from which God communed with Moses, and where the blood was placed by the high priest for the sins of the people once each year.

Solomon built this temple in Jerusalem, which God had chosen as His city. It stood on the level top of God's mountain with a magnificent view of the surrounding city and countryside. It was the pride of Israel, and all men were required to come to it on three feast days each year to worship God in His place of residence.

But unless God lives in men's hearts, they cannot find Him in a structure. After Solomon's death, two of his sons split the kingdom. Quickly the northern kingdom of Israel forgot Yahweh, and began to worship the Canaanite gods, and made images of golden calves, and worshipped them. They gathered in groves of trees and worshipped Baal and passed their children through the fire as sacrifices.

In 2 Kings 17:18 we are told their fate: "Therefore the Lord was very angry with Israel, and removed them out of his sight: there was none left but the tribe of Judah only." God allowed the Assyrians to destroy the tribes of Israel for their wickedness, leaving only the southern kingdom of Judah. In Jerusalem, the capital, stood His temple; yet in spite of that magnificent building, Judah also forgot the Lord.

Destruction of the First Temple

God, through His servants the prophets, had told them what He would do, but they hadn't paid attention. Judah had turned away from the Lord and committed sins that were as bad or worse than the northern kingdom's sins. Far away, in the land along the Euphrates River, the Lord raised up a nation to bring down Judah and punish them. In fact, they would be taken away captive out of the land which God had given to their fathers.

Nebuchadnezzar, king of Babylon, came first in about 600 B.C. and reduced Judah to a vassal state, paying tribute to the Babylonians in return for their safety. But when Jehoiakim refused to pay this tribute in 598 B.C. the Babylonian armies were on the march again. By the following year Jerusalem had been taken and the Babylonians began to again transport Hebrews out of their homeland to relocate them in Babylon.

This was the time of the prophets Daniel and Ezekiel who had been carried away to this new land, and of Jeremiah who remained in Judah, calling on his countrymen not to resist the invading Babylonians — for God had sent them in punishment for their sins. Jeremiah's admonishment went unheeded, and he was badly treated by his own people.

Then on the ninth day of the month of Ab, the Babylonian troops set fire to Solomon's Temple and destroyed it. They pulled down the building stones and left only an area of charred rubble where the house of God once stood.

The Babylonian Captivity

Jeremiah told them exactly how long their captivity in Babylon would last. In Jeremiah 25:11 we read, "And this whole land shall be a desolation, and an astonishment; and these nations shall serve the king of Babylon seventy years."

It had not been God's plan for permanent exile of His people, and He was raising another nation and another man who would allow them to return. In 539 B.C. Babylon fell to the Persians without a fight, and Cyrus, king of Persia, took control. The amazing thing is that the Bible contains prophecy, written by Isaiah over a century before, which not only tells us what this man would do — but actually calls him *by name*. "That saith of Cyrus, He is my shepherd, and shall perform all my pleasure: even saying to Jerusalem, Thou shalt be built; and to the temple, Thy foundation shall be laid" (Isa. 44:28).

The next chapter of Isaiah tells us more about the Lord's plans for Cyrus, and how he would rule the greatest empire of his time. But the Lord had also prepared this man's heart in a very special way which would affect the fate of the Hebrews captive in the land he had just conquered.

In a world where every nation of people, with the exception of the Hebrews, were polytheistic, worshipping many gods, Cyrus came under the influence of a small sect founded by Zoroaster which taught that there was only *one* God. Although this religion had elements which were different from Judaism, there was so much similarity that when Cyrus heard of the captive people who also believed in only one God, he immediately felt a closeness to these Hebrews.

That God's hand was on Cyrus is very evident from incidents in his life. In fact, his own grandfather ordered his death as soon as he was born, but the man assigned to slay the child could not find it in his heart to do it. Cyrus was spared by what may be called the divine intervention of God, and lived to fulfill all that had been prophesied about him. In a time when monarchs were savage and cruel, Cyrus was an enlightened and benevolent ruler. A year after he had captured the city of Babylon, he issued an edict which allowed all Hebrews to return to their homeland if they desired to. He supplied them with food, goods, and the money necessary to rebuild the temple.

After all the years in Babylon, many Hebrews — now called Jews, after Judea — were comfortable in this new land and refused to leave. In 536 B.C. less than fifty thousand returned to Jerusalem under Zerubbabel, the grandson of King Jehoiachin. The foundation of the new temple was laid the following year, but construction stopped when the workmen came under attack by the Samaritans. It was finally completed in 515 B.C. under the direction of Haggai.

It was not until 445 B.C. when Nehemiah rebuilt the walls,

that Jerusalem was again safe from the Samaritan attacks, and it is this time in which the animosity between Jews and Samaritans began which is evident in Jesus' ministry.

The Second Temple

The structure built by the returned Hebrews could in no way compare with the magnificent Temple of Solomon, but they did the best they could with the meager resources at their disposal. For the very few whose eyes had actually beheld the former splendor, it was a great disappointment.

When King Solomon had begun, he had in gold alone the equivalent in today's money of over ten billion dollars. This was just for the lining of the walls, and the vessels and utensils for servicing the temple. He also had in silver the equivalent of over one hundred million dollars. All told, Solomon's Temple probably could not be duplicated today for any less than one hundred billion dollars.

The second temple was completed, and worship began again in the house of the Lord in Jerusalem. As generations passed the population grew; and the decades faded into centuries until a new world conqueror came upon the scene to defeat the Persians.

The rise of this man, Alexander, had also been prophesied. Daniel foretold the coming of a king from Greece who would wrest control of the land of the Persians and forge his own mighty empire. After defeating Darius III at Issus in 333 B.C. he led his army south to conquer Egypt. On the way he took the fortress at Gaza, and personally detoured to visit Jerusalem. Although nothing of this period is told in the Bible, Josephus gives us a detailed account.[1]

When Jaddua, the high priest, heard that Alexander was coming, he was terrified, expecting the city to be sacked and the temple treasures confiscated. But God told Jaddua not to worry. He and the citizens of Jerusalem were to wear robes of white and to open the gates to greet Alexander.

God also sent a dream to the Macedonian king, and when Alexander approached the gates of Jerusalem he saw the faces he had seen in his dream — wearing the same white robes as in that dream. Jaddua's face he especially recognized, as the high priest welcomed him to the city.

Alexander entered the temple and offered a sacrifice to God, telling the priests that as a boy God had appeared to him in a vision and told him of his future conquests. When Alexander was shown the prophecies concerning himself in the Book of Daniel, he was convinced that the God of the Hebrews was the same as in his vision. Nothing was plundered in the city, and not a shekel taken from the Lord's treasury by Alexander. Instead he promised special treatment for all Jews throughout the lands which he would conquer.

Alexander did indeed go on to many victories, and his empire stretched from Egypt to India. But in June of 323 B.C. Alexander the Great died, leaving his empire to "the strongest." His generals proceeded to carve up the lands.

Two of these generals and the territories they and their descendents controlled were to have dire consequences for the Jews. To the north was Syria and their Seleucid rulers. To the south in Egypt the Ptolemaic kingdom posed an immediate threat. In 320 B.C. Ptolemy I marched into Judea and annexed it. The years to come would find Judea almost continually fought over by the Seleucids and Ptolemies, and control of Jerusalem went back and forth between them.

It was not until the rise of yet another eventual world conqueror, Rome, and a brief period of Judean independence, that the Jews could breathe easily — for a short time.

The Judeans sent a delegation to Rome and requested to be placed under Rome's protection. This was granted, although at the time the Jews received little in benefit from this alliance. Rome was busy expanding an empire and the affairs of an obscure backwater territory was not of urgent priority. Jerusalem was looted several times, twice by the Romans themselves.

In 63 B.C. the Roman general Pompey defeated the Seleucids and continued into Palestine, and Judea officially became a Roman province. With this, the political independence of this nation came to an abrupt halt. Their "protectors" had become their masters.

Pompey attempted a revolt against Julius Caesar, was defeated, and fled into Egypt. Caesar's legions followed and their route into Egypt was through Palestine. An Idumaean governor of Galilee, Antipater, came to Caesar's assistance with men and supplies, and after Caesar returned from Egypt he was made procurator of all Judea. In 43 B.C. Antipater died, and his son was confirmed as the governor of Judea. This young man's name was Herod, later to be called "the Great."

Herod Enlarges the Temple

There is certainly not space here to tell more than a few details of the life and deeds of Herod the Great. This man who ruled the Jews in Palestine was himself not even a Jew. He had ten wives and at least fifty children. His paranoid personality caused him to suspect even his sons of plotting against him, and he had all but four of them executed. This is the Herod who ordered the massacre of the male Hebrew children in and around Bethlehem to rid himself of the baby Jesus, whom the Magi had come to find as the newborn "King of the Jews."

Herod was hated by his subjects. He neither understood nor appreciated their religion. Although he had to conform to many Jewish dietary laws and customs, Herod loved the worldly style of Greek life which the Romans had appropriated as their own. He married a Hebrew royal princess and later killed her with his own hand. But this man was obsessed with raising Palestine out of its rural and unsophisticated status and into the modern world. He intended to accomplish this by a series of immense construction projects.

To pacify his subjects, he decided to restore the temple to its original splendor. Not with his own money, of course. The people would be heavily taxed to pay for it.

To accommodate his grandiose plans, Herod enlarged the top of Mount Moriah by constructing a wall along its edge and filling it with rock. Beginning in 20 B.C. and employing ten thousand workmen and stone masons, the entire reconstruction took eighty years to finally complete. But in Jesus' time, the temple was indeed magnificent.

The main entry was through the Golden Gate through doors of brass that were so massive that twenty men were required to open or shut them. This gate let to the Court of the Gentiles, beyond which none but Jews could proceed on penalty of death. Through the Beautiful Gate was the Court of the Women and the Treasury. This was as far as women were permitted to go.

Beyond this was the Gate of Nicanor leading to the Court

of the Men. Finally there was the splendid Court of the Priests where the sacrifices were offered at the four-cornered Altar of Burnt Offering. Here the temple choir and the musicians led the singing and chanting of prayers and psalms. But the most beautiful structure lay beyond this, the temple itself.

The heart of all this magnificence was the Holy of Holies, which was actually very small. This structure of pure white stone and gold was 120 feet wide, with its double doors covered with a veil of rich purple and blue material. Inside were the tables of Shewbread, the seven-branched Menorah, and the Altar of Incense. Beyond this was a smaller room separated by a veil of beautiful cloth. This was empty, except for a stone which represented the ark of the covenant — lost since the destruction of the first temple. This Holiest of Holies was entered only once each year by the high priest on the Day of Atonement. It was only in this room and only on this one day that he was permitted to speak aloud the sacred name of Yahweh.

It was not only on the Temple Mount that Herod's construction could be seen. Walls around the city rose 250 feet above the valley below. On the northwest side of the temple wall was the Tower of Antonia, each of its four corner turrets nearly 120 feet high. Herod's palace was visible at the city's highest point near the west wall, surrounded by three more imposing towers.

But the crowning glory of Jerusalem was the Tabernacle of the Temple. Josephus, who was a Jew born in this land, describes this pure white building as "like a snowcapped mountain." Of all of Herod's ambitious construction projects, this was indeed his greatest architectural achievement.

The Destruction of the Second Temple

When Jesus prophesied the destruction of this magnificent structure, Herod the Great had already been dead for thirty-seven years. The finishing touches on some of it had not yet been completed, and work would continue for another thirty years.

A few days before He was crucified, Jesus was in the temple with His disciples. Matthew 24:1-2 tells us, "And Jesus went out, and departed from the temple: and his disciples came to him for to shew him the buildings of the temple. And Jesus said unto them, See ye not all these things? verily I say unto you, There shall not be left here one stone upon another, that shall not be thrown down."

Luke quotes Jesus warning Jerusalem of what will happen: "And when ye shall see Jerusalem compassed with armies, then know that the desolation thereof is nigh" (Luke 21:20).

The events leading up to the fulfillment of Jesus' prophecy began in May of A.D. 66. The Zealots had been increasing their protests against the Romans, and were killing them whenever an opportunity presented itself. But when the Roman procurator Florus demanded the keepers of the temple treasury to pay him seventeen talents of gold, open revolt broke out.

The Roman garrison was seized by the Zealots and the entire county was in turmoil. Gallus, the Roman governor of Syria, sent a legion of soldiers to put down the revolt, but was forced back with heavy losses. Nero appointed a veteran commander, Vespasian, to deal with these upstart Jews. With three of Rome's best legions, Vespasian and his son Titus marched on Palestine. Before Vespasian could complete his mission Nero was assassinated, and the general was summoned to Rome without delay.

In the spring of A.D. 70 Titus surrounded Jerusalem with his army of about 80,000 men. The city was swarming with people, for many had come to celebrate Passover — war or not — and were trapped inside. The siege lasted until July, with bloody fighting, sickness, and starvation.

Josephus, who had been captured early in the war by the Romans, was an eyewitness to the end. Titus had ordered that the sanctuary of the temple be spared, but one of his soldiers threw a blazing torch through the Golden Window that opened into the rooms next to the Holy of Holies. These rooms, which were paneled with wood and contained the jars of holy oil, burst into flames. Titus ordered the fire to be extinguished, but his men, bent on seizing as many of the valuable objects as possible, ignored his order. The Holy Place went up in flames. Later, Titus commanded that the whole city, including the temple, be razed to the ground. All he spared were Herod's towers, which were necessary to garrison his troops.

The second temple was destroyed on the ninth day of the month of Ab. Josephus remarks in wonder at the timing of this destruction, for it was on exactly the same day of the same month as the destruction of the first temple, built by Solomon.[2]

The prophecy made by Jesus, thirty-seven years before, had also been fulfilled. One Roman centurian was heard to say that there was not one stone left upon another, and that there was no sign that the place had ever been inhabited.

The simple probability of these two events happening on exactly the same day does not reflect the *improbability* of these events — separated by almost seven centuries — happening on the same day. Here again, I believe God is demonstrating His complete and total control over the destiny of mankind and the events of history.

How can anyone *not* recognize this?

19

Can the Trinity Be Explained?

Perhaps the most difficult concept of Christianity to explain is the mystery of the Trinity. How can our God exist in three separate and distinct persons: Father, Son, and Holy Spirit, yet be one God?

If Christians find it hard to grasp this possibility, imagine the problem it presents for those of other faiths. Moslems, in particular, cannot understand how Christians can profess to believe that there is only *one* God, yet worship Him as *three* individual beings. They claim that Christianity is not monotheistic, but polytheistic.

Can our belief in the Trinity be explained in understandable terms?

Perhaps it can!

The Mystery of the Trinity

The Bible tells us in Genesis 1:1 that in the beginning, it was God who created the heaven and the earth. This can only mean that *before* this time of creation, only God existed. Nothing of what our universe is comprised of was in existence before then. He was responsible for creation.

We are also told in Isaiah 43:10 that there is only one God: "Before me there was no God formed, neither shall there be after me."

The angels who serve God are created beings, and were not pre-existent. This is evident from Ezekiel 28:15 where God is talking about Satan. "Thou wast perfect in thy ways from the day that thou wast created, till iniquity was found in thee."

Since Satan and the other heavenly beings were *created* by God, it is evident that at one time *only* God existed. These created beings are *not* deity, and are not part of the Godhead. Their power comes *from* God, and what they can and cannot do is strictly prescribed by God's permission and by His supreme authority. But what about the other two persons of the Trinity? Is there any scriptural evidence that they *pre-existed* before creation?

There can be no dispute, of course, that God the Father, is truly God, but the mystery of the Trinity also includes God the Son and God the Holy Spirit. Were they also pre-existent before creation?

John 1:1 tells us: "In the beginning was the Word, and the Word was with God, and the Word was God." There is no doubt about whom John was speaking, for in John 1:14 he says, "And the Word was made flesh, and dwelt among us." The Word was Jesus Christ, the Son of God.

Was the Son present at creation? John 1:3 tells us that He was. "All things were made by him; and without him was not any thing made that was made."

Jesus, the Son of God, was present at creation, therefore He was pre-existent with God *before* creation.

The third person of the Trinity was also present at creation, for in Genesis 1:2 we are told, "And the spirit of God moved upon the face of the waters." The Holy Spirit, therefore, was also pre-existent before creation, and is also deity.

By scriptural testimony it can be established that *all three* of the persons of the Trinity were present at creation, and thereby *pre-existent*. Since only God was pre-existent, then it follows that *all three* are indeed God.

The hidden numerical design found in the Bible also bears witness to this. We have seen in a previous chapter where God has placed a "numerical fingerprint" throughout the Hebrew of the Old Testament and the Greek of the New Testament to give irrefutable evidence of the authenticity of these manuscripts as His Word. Let us briefly examine this as it pertains to the three persons of the Trinity.

God	37 X 15	τ͑ου Θεου'
Godhead	37 X 26	Θεοτητος

Jesus	37 X 24	Ιησους
Christ	37 X 40	Χριστον"
Holy Spirit	37 X 44	αγιου πνευματος
Spirit	37 X 32	πνευματος

Jesus commanded His disciples to baptize believers in the names of all *three persons* of the Trinity. In Matthew 28:19 He instructed them, "Go ye therefore, and teach all nations, baptizing them in the name of the Father, and of the Son, and of the Holy Ghost." Since God has stated clearly that He will *not* share His glory with anyone, it is clear that *all three* persons of the Trinity are really *one,* the Godhead.

The mystery of the Trinity, the concept that God can be one, yet exist in three separate and distinct persons is beyond the comprehension of our limited, mortal minds. We who are confined to understanding only what our earthly existence allows us to personally experience, cannot easily come to terms with this possibility.

I have been asked many times to try to explain the mystery of the Trinity by people who could either not understand it, or because of its complicated and ambiguous nature — refused to accept it. I tried the best I could to do this, pointing out that although all three persons of the Trinity shared all of God's attributes, God the Father exemplified the holiness of the Godhead; Jesus demonstrated the personality of God; while the Holy Spirit manifested the awesome power of the Almighty.

For some it may have served as a satisfactory explanation, but I knew that for others it did not. Of course there was more to the Trinity — much more — than my meager words could possibly convey, but I was unable to explain this more appropriately.

Then one day as I stood by the shore of the sea I was suddenly struck by something wonderfully similar — something which could possibly make others understand as never before.

Understanding the Trinity

As you stand by the shore of the sea, as far as your eyes can see — and beyond — is the mighty ocean. It is an entity of enormous power, sometimes as still and calm as a tropical pool, sometimes rising in fury to smash those who dare to intrude upon it.

As you observe, a swell of water rises offshore. The wave gathers momentum as it approaches the beach. Although it remains a part of the sea it has a life of its own. Then, after crashing high upon the shore, it returns to the sea from which it came. As a wave it had its own identity, but *never* was it separate from the sea.

Just as Jesus came from the Father and returned to the Father, He had — and still has — an identity of His own. The wave was never separate from the sea, just as Jesus was never separate from the Father. Just as the wave exemplifies the personality of the sea, Jesus *is* the personality of God the Father. If you have seen a wave, then you *must* have seen the sea. If you have seen Jesus, you have also seen the Father.

And as you stand beside the shore, you become aware of another part of the sea. The salt air which invigorates you is also an integral part of the sea. It, too, has a separate existence from the sea, but is very much *one* with it. It penetrates everywhere and everything within miles of the coastline. As you approach the beach it is the signal that the sea is not far away. In fact, it *is* the sea — reaching out to you through the air.

This is exactly what the Holy Spirit does. Just as the salt air draws men to the sea, the Holy Spirit draws men to the Father through Jesus Christ. The Spirit, although having a separate existence, is *not* separate from the Godhead.

I have used this simple example for several years now. People seem to be able to understand better the concept of the Trinity through the parallel relationship of sea and wave and salt air representing the Father, Son, and Holy Spirit than by any of my previous attempts to explain it.

Children, especially, are quick to grasp the meaning of this "parable" approach to the mystery of the Trinity. I suppose we older and more sophisticated adults should not be totally surprised at this. After all, the Bible tells us that "a little child shall lead them."

20

Where Is Heaven? — and Hell? Has Science Located Them?

A Soviet cosmonaut, after returning from space, sarcastically remarked, "I looked around for God up there, but I didn't see Him."

This man, like many others, equates the word "heaven" to mean the area in our physical world above the earth. God is indeed in heaven, but His heaven is not a part of what man can experience in our own universe, confined to the dimensions which dictate our temporal experience, and progressing along an additional dimension which we call "time."

The fact that heaven is invisible to us certainly does *not* mean that it does not exist any more than the fact that God is invisible means that *He* does not exist. The evidence of God's reality is all around us manifested in His creation.

But where *is* heaven?

Can science possibly explain where it *might* be located?

I think that perhaps it can!

This chapter will be very difficult for many readers to fully understand. It will present a concept that, to my knowledge, has never before been formally presented. I admit that it contains speculation, but I also believe that it may offer the solution to something which has troubled and confused man throughout the ages — the physical location of heaven and hell.

I will try to make this difficult subject matter as clear as possible, and give applicable references from Scripture to substantiate my conclusions.

The Breakthrough

In August of 1984 a pair of physicists, John Schwarz and Michael Green,[1] sat at a desk in Aspen, Colorado. These men had been working on a theory which had required them to perform the most complicated mathematics they had ever done. Now they were down to the final calculation, a simple multiplication of 31 times sixteen. If the answer was 496, their mathematics were correct. Michael Green scribbled the numbers on the blackboard — 496. The mathematics of their theory had proven to be correct.

They had been working on a mathematical equation which incorporates all four natural forces in the universe: gravity, electromagnetic, and the strong and weak nuclear forces. Their theory was based on a strange concept of the universe, that the fundamental building blocks of matter and energy are not infinitesimal points, but infinitesimal strings.

But the astonishing part of this mathematical equation was that it contained not just the *three* physical dimensions, plus "time," but a total of *ten* dimensions.[2]

Gary Taubes, in an excellent article about this published in *Discover Magazine*,[3] says that "No theory in the past fifty years has elicited so much excitement and optimism. Physicists, usually a reticent bunch, now unabashedly talk of a revolution. They compare the breakthrough in superstrings to the birth of quantum physics or Einstein's creation of general relativity. They say the mathematics behind superstrings is so compelling that you have to believe."

Edward Witten of Princeton says, "It's beautiful, wonderful, majestic — and strange, if you like, but it's not weird."

The search for a mathematical equation expressing all four primary forces of physics began with Einstein himself, after he had developed his general and special theories of relativity. But in all the years that this great mathematician tried to find the answer, he failed to find a single set of equations that show the four fundamental forces to be separate manifestations of one even more fundamental force. What Einstein was not able to accomplish, Schwarz and Green have succeeded in doing.

Others had also tried, but found that their equations contained either "infinities" — a number divided by zero; or "anomalies," which result in negative probability of an event happening. In the Schwarz and Green equations, the infinities cancelled themselves out — almost miraculously — and were free of anomalies. It also had much in common with some theories which had already been suggested on the basis of observational experiment.

But how do these sets of complicated mathematical equations fit with the location of heaven and hell?

Our Universe

Everything in the universe we are a part of is built on the basis of three physical dimensions, plus the additional dimension of time. Let us briefly examine what this means.

We start with a simple point which mathematicians call a singularity. A point has no dimensions, it's just there. But if we move that point, we form a line — which has only one dimension. We will call that dimension — *length.*

If we add another line at a right angle to the first line, we are describing a plane, which has two dimensions — length and width.

Now if we add a third line, perpendicular to the first two, we are adding the third dimension — height, and have a solid object — which is the basis of our universe of *three* physical dimensions.

Einstein's theory of general relativity placed the additional dimension of time in our universe, which makes sense. In order to say where something is, you have to specify the element of when it was there.

So we are confined to these three dimensions of length, width, and height — plus an additional required dimension of time. These four dimensions describe *everything* that we are aware of in our physical universe.

In our world every bit of matter and energy is governed by the four fundamental forces which operate in the three physical dimensions in which we are enclosed. These three dimensions are our boundaries, and we cannot escape from them. Everything from a single atom within our own bodies to an exploding supernova a billion light years from the earth is confined within these limiting dimensions.

This is *our* world, but in John 18:36, Jesus answered Pilate's question by saying, "My kingdom is not of this world."

God is certainly *not* confined to only our dimensional

limitations. In 2 Chronicles 2:6 we read Solomon's reflection on the magnitude of God, "But who is able to build him an house, seeing the heaven and heaven of heavens cannot contain him?"

We find right in His Word, a reference to the fact that God's kingdom — heaven — is *not* of this world, and that even the heaven of heavens cannot contain Him, for He transcends all physical limitations.

From this we can conclude that since God's abode of heaven is not located within the three dimensional limits of our world, then it must be located *outside* of it.

Heaven's Location

Michael Green concluded a lecture with the question, "Is there some deep geometrical reason why in ten dimensions this theory is special?"

I believe there may be an answer to this question in the location of two "other worlds" which the Bible emphatically states are in existence. One of these is "heaven," the dwelling place of God and the destination of those who have accepted Jesus Christ as Saviour and Lord.

Our universe is structured on three physical dimensions, plus the additional dimension of time. There is no way that our particular dimensions may be extended *outside* of our universe, but suppose the dimension of time is transcendent — not limited to our own universe — and shared mutually by worlds outside of our own. If, as calculations indicate, there is a total of ten possible dimensions, if we subtract the three that define our universe, plus time, that leaves six dimensions left over.

Three of the remaining dimensions *could* be the location of heaven.

Since each of these "heavenly" dimensions would be at right angles to those of our own, *heaven could occupy exactly the same space as our own world does.*

In other words, it is mathematically possible that the earth and heaven exist simultaneously in the same space, but with dimensions at right angles to each other. It is impossible for us to visualize this mentally, for we are conditioned to think only in the dimensions of our own universe, but this is mathematically possible.

Consider for a moment how this would help to explain many of the supernatural events described in the Bible, such as the sudden and unexpected appearance of an angel.

Let's look at some Scripture and consider it in the light of what we have just discussed. We know that when Jesus was born into this world He possessed a body exactly like our own. Jesus was "made flesh," just as we are. His body at that time was limited to the constrictions of our own dimensional universe. But *after* the Resurrection, *after* He had ascended to His Father, He returned to earth again to appear before His disciples. Look at what the Bible tells us about that meeting.

The disciples were together in a room in Jerusalem with the door closed. Then suddenly He was with them. "And as they thus spake, Jesus himself stood in the midst of them, and saith unto them, Peace be unto you" (Luke 24:36).

Jesus had *suddenly* appeared! He had entered a room through either the walls or a closed door. Jesus had passed through the physical matter which makes up our world. How could He have accomplished this?

I believe the explanation is that He entered the room by passing from the dimensions of heaven to the dimensions of our world. His body was no longer restricted by the limitations of our earthly bodies, but could pass from one set of dimensions to another.

The Bible tells us of the sudden appearance of angels. Mary was visited by Gabriel who informed her that she would bear the Son of God. Zacharias was confronted by the angel of the Lord within the temple and was told that his wife would give birth to a child whose name was to be John. Lot was visited by angels before the destruction of Sodom. These created beings suddenly appear as though they had passed through an invisible wall from *another world.*

In Genesis 5:24 we are told, "And Enoch walked with God: and he was not; for God took him." Enoch was suddenly translated through that invisible wall leading to another entirely different set of physical dimensions.

Elijah was taken into heaven by what appeared to Elisha to be a whirlwind. Elijah also passed through the constrictions of our physical world and entered heaven.

When Jesus ascended into heaven from the Mount of Olives, His disciples saw Him pass from our world into another. "And it came to pass, while he blessed them, he was parted from them, and carried up into heaven" (Luke 24:51).

In each case where angels appear or disappear, they do so suddenly — as though they pass into an unseen place which co-exists with our own world. When Enoch and Elijah were translated they were not taken off into outer space, but vanished while they were still within the earth's atmosphere. Jesus was taken up into the clouds, which are a part of our own world, when He was taken into heaven. In each and every one of these events described in the Bible, the person *just vanished*.

How might this be scientifically explained? Do the set of equations found by Schwarz and Green provide an answer to this?

Yes, they do!

Not only do the equations prescribe a total of nine physical dimensions, plus the transcendent dimension of time, it also *connects* all of these physical dimensions with what are called "strings." In this system each dimension would interface others by an infinite number of infinitesimally small pathways. The equations allow the possibility of energy and matter to sometimes pass through these minute channels from one set of dimensions to another.

Our earthly bodies, of course, cannot do this, but the mathematics allow for the possibility of something similar to what happens in the science fiction films *Star Trek* when Mr. Spock says, "Beam me up, Scotty."

The Location of Hell

I do not believe that it is an accident that the equations indicate the possibility of *three* sets of three dimensions each, plus the transcendent dimension of time.[4] I don't think it was strange that in these equations the infinities and anomalies *all* cancelled out. It is not surprising to me that these equations are almost universally described as "beautiful mathematics." The reason for this, I believe, is that the equations are correct.

We have accounted for two sets of three dimensions each: our world, and heaven, plus the dimension of time which is universally shared by all others. This leaves us with three more physical dimensions unaccounted for. These three form an entirely separate and distinct additional "world," a world which we call *hell*.

In the sixteenth chapter of Luke, Jesus relates a parable which confirms this. He is telling about the beggar, Lazarus, who sat at a rich man's gate. Lazarus died and was taken to Abraham's bosom by angels. The rich man also died, and in hell he lifted up his eyes and saw Lazarus. He implored Abraham to let Lazarus come to him with water to cool his torment in the flames.

Abraham refused, and told him, "And beside all this, between us and you there is a great gulf fixed: so that they which would pass from hence to you cannot; neither can they pass to us, that would come from thence" (Luke 16:26).

There was a physical barrier between paradise and hell, which can be explained in terms of these two places existing in separate sets of dimensions. To go between these was not possible for the souls of men. The Bible tells us that during the time between His crucifixion and resurrection, Jesus descended into hades to preach, but Jesus, being God, could do anything He pleased without restriction.

In 1 Peter 3:18-20 we are told of this: "... being put to death in the flesh, but quickened by the Spirit: By which also he went and preached unto the spirits in prison; Which sometime were disobedient, when once the long-suffering of God waited in the days of Noah, while the ark was a preparing, wherein few, that is, eight souls were saved by water."

I rather doubt that the souls of those in hell can look up and see those who are in heaven. I also doubt that those souls in heaven can see relatives and loved ones suffering the torment of hell. But Jesus was making a point in this parable — that in the after-life, once a destination has been determined, a soul cannot change that judgment. It is permanent, fixed, and for all eternity.

The location of hell, therefore, is in another set of physical dimensions which co-exists in the same *space* as our present physical world and, hopefully, our future home — heaven.

But what about the mystery of a person's soul itself? Can these mathematical equations give us any information concerning our souls?

The Soul

First we must examine what a soul really is. It cannot be seen, it has no weight, no color, no physical property which can be measured. None of our sophisticated scientific instruments can even detect its existence. But we know instinctively that the soul is a part of every man, woman, and child on earth. But *what* is it, and *where* is it?

In Genesis 2:7 we are told, "And the Lord God formed man of the dust of the ground, and breathed into his nostrils the breath of life; and man became a living soul."

If a soul has no *physical* characteristics, then how can we possess it, for we are physical beings? Can something outside of the boundaries of the dimensions which define our universe actually be a part of us? The answer to this question and to an understanding of our souls may be found by looking closely at what comprises a physical object.

For anything to be physical in our universe, it must be solid. To be solid it must have three dimensions. But *must* the soul have all three of the dimensions of this universe?

We have already determined that a line has only the dimension of length. In our physical universe a line does not really exist. We know that it is there, but we cannot see it, for it has no thickness. We may be able to measure the distance of a line between two points, but we actually cannot see the line itself. If we draw a line with a pencil, what we see is the three dimensional graphite we used to *indicate* the line.

If we have two lines intersecting at right angles we have a plane. We can see a plane which makes up a surface because it is part of a three dimensional solid object. But we really cannot see a plane, because it consists of only *two* dimensions.

Two separate and distinct "worlds" can exist in the same space because their dimensions are at right angles to each other. But in geometric arrangement it is possible that these worlds could *share* one common dimension. The other world would be completely unseen and undetectable by the other, for the shared dimension would be a line, and we have just determined that a line which exists by itself is invisible and would not be detectable.

Suppose that a soul would have one dimension in common with our physical world, while the other two of its dimensions were not. It would be connected to our world by an invisible dimension: undetectable by our scientific methods. But *it would exist!*

The soul would exist because it had three dimensions, even if one of these was shared between two separate worlds. It could be a mirror image of ourselves, a part of ourselves, yet completely undiscernible physically within this world.

Let us look at an example of something similar. Let us say that you are six feet tall, with broad shoulders, but were as thin as the gossamer strand of a spider's web. If you were to stand near a wall in the sunshine you would cast a shadow on the wall — if you stood facing it. But if you turn sideways, the shadow you would cast on the wall would be virtually invisible. This is similar to the "shadow" which a soul would cast, except that it would be *entirely* invisible.

Do our souls exist in limbo, partly in this world and partly in another? At death the soul would be free from the body of which it was a part, and exist completely in the other world. Then, subject to God's judgment, the final destination of the soul would be determined.

In Luke 12:20 Jesus tells of the rich man who built larger barns to store his goods, but neglected the state of his soul. But one night his life was over and God told him, "Thou fool, this night thy soul shall be required of thee."

We are given a picture of the judgment of souls which is to come: ". . . and he shall separate them one from another, as a shepherd divideth his sheep from the goats: And he shall set the sheep on his right hand, but the goats on the left. Then shall the King say unto them on his right hand, Come, ye blessed of my Father, inherit the kingdom prepared for you from the foundation of the world" (Matt. 25:32-34). But in Matthew 25:41 He speaks regarding the goats: "Depart from me, ye cursed, into everlasting fire."

From this it is evident that souls will be judged: the righteous to reward and the evil to eternal torment. These two places, heaven and hell, are separated by an impenetrable gulf of totally different dimensions.

Mathematics — A Window to the Supernatural

Mathematics is the only *pure* science. It is exact, precise, and unequivocal. It transcends space, time, and dimensions. If the proper values are used in an equation and the arithmetic is correct, the answer will always be exactly the same.

In any part of our universe, or in any other conceivable universe, 2 + 2 will always equal 4. It makes no difference what language is spoken, or what the units of measurement are called, or the base on which the mathematics is calculated, mathematics is universal — and beyond.

To try to contact life elsewhere in our own universe, the numerical equivalent of pi, the numerical value of the ratio of the circumference of a circle to its diameter, 3.1416, is transmitted by radio into space. Any life sufficiently intelligent to have a radio receiver, would immediately recognize this number and realize that another intelligent life form was transmitting it. This value of pi would hold true in any other universe outside of our own.

Mathematics then, transcends all dimensions. If the four fundamental forces of *our* natural world are also the fundamental forces of worlds *outside* our own, then a mathematical equation could conceivably give us valuable information of the likelihood of other worlds existing.

This is exactly what the set of equations written by Schwarz and Green may be doing. I believe that through the "window" provided by these particular equations, we have been able to confirm by science what the Bible has said all along — that beside this world we live in are two other worlds — heaven and hell. The fact that these equations predict *exactly ten dimensions* is precisely in line with Scripture.

Let us briefly compare what the science of mathematics now tells us with what the Bible has been saying all along.

> • The Bible says that in addition to this world, there is a real physical heaven and a real physical hell. These equations say that a total of ten dimensions exist. Our universe is bounded by three, leaving three for heaven and three for hell. With the dimension of time shared by all, this coincides exactly with the biblical account of three separate and distinct worlds.
> • The Bible tells us that we each have a soul which will survive the death of our bodies. These equations show that the geometric position of three sets of dimensions allow for a soul to co-exist in two dimensions of two separate worlds at the same time.
> • The Bible tells us that Enoch and Elijah were taken physically to heaven. These equations indicate the possibility of such translations.
> • The Bible tells of the sudden appearance and disappearance of angels. These equations allow this

through the interconnecting "strings" between two separate worlds.

• The Bible indicates that Jesus was taken up into heaven at a close distance from the earth's surface. These equations allow all three worlds to occupy the same physical space.

The Significance of This

Although science has proven the Bible to be correct in much of what it tells us about events which happened in our *natural* world, until now it has not been able to corroborate the Bible's references to the *supernatural*, including the existence of heaven and hell as actual places outside of the world in which we now live. Nor could it comment on the scientific possibility of man really having what the Bible calls a "soul."

Now, through the science of mathematics, there is evidence for the existence of two other "worlds" or universes beside our own, separated by two entirely different sets of three dimensions each. It is tremendously significant that these equations define only ten dimensions. Why only ten? Why not eight, or fourteen, or an infinite number of them? The reason is that God did not *need* any more!

The Bible tells us that there are only three possible habitations for man. We live at present in one and our eternity will be spent in either heaven or in hell. God, the Creator, had no use at all for any other possible worlds and did not create them.

For the first time, through mathematics, science has provided a means by which we may see beyond the limiting dimensions of this world, and find proof that what the Bible tells us exists beyond the grave is really there and scientifically possible.

These beautiful sets of equations have been called by some "The Theory of Everything."

It may well be!

21

Has God Already Turned Off the Sun? Scientific Evidence Says Maybe!

In Matthew 24:29 Jesus makes an astonishing statement: "Immediately after the tribulation of those days shall the sun be darkened, and the moon shall not give her light." Bible scholars have puzzled over this for centuries. What does this mean? Will the sun really be turned down so that less sunlight will reach the earth? Perhaps some recent scientific evidence will help us to understand this amazing statement — made by Jesus — who certainly should know exactly what will happen in the end times.

To explain this scientific discovery we will first have to review a bit about what we know of our sun and the fusion process which powers it. Until recently the source of the sun's power was a mystery. It was not until science duplicated the sun's solar furnace with the fusion of hydrogen, first in the hydrogen bomb and later in preliminary experiments with hydrogen fusion as a source of useful energy, that the mechanism of what is happening in the interior of the sun and other stars was understood.

The sun is a ball of hot gasses 865,000 miles in diameter, 109 times the diameter of the earth. The great size of the sun means that near the center there is extremely high gravitational pressure, forcing the nuclei of the hydrogen atoms close together. The forces of gravity generate extreme heat, and the protons of the hydrogen atoms actually form a plasma. It is within this high temperature plasma that four nuclei combine to form an atom of helium — with the release of tremendous energy.

Within the core of the sun the energy produced is equivalent to *90 billion one-megaton hydrogen bombs exploding every second*. The physical conditions produced by this are beyond our imagination. Temperatures are in the tens of millions of degrees and a pressure over 200 billion times that which we experience in the earth's atmosphere. Each second 700 million tons of hydrogen are consumed — converted to helium — with the release of all types of particles and radiation, as mass is converted to energy.

What we see and feel on earth is sunlight. It is the steady bombardment of photons of light which make life possible on our planet. Without this sunlight life could not exist. But the sunlight we see and feel today on earth was produced within the core of the sun about a million years ago. Due to the extreme gravitational field of the sun, the photons of light take that long to reach the sun's exterior. Then, within a little over eight minutes, traveling at 186,000 miles per second, the million-year-old photons of light arrive on earth.

When we look at our sun (through a dark lens — not unprotected eyes), we can see only the surface. Until recently we had no way of knowing just what was taking place in the sun's interior. Since the sunlight reaching the earth is about a million years old, there was no means by which we could determine what was happening *right now* in the sun's nuclear fusion furnace.

But now there is, and what we have learned is startling. In 1930 a new sub-atomic particle had been postulated by Wolfgang Pauli. During experiments he found that something was carrying energy away from nuclear disintegrations and it would have to be a new particle with no electrical charge. He named this new particle the neutrino, which means "little neutral one."

Because the neutrino was so small and carried no electrical charge, it was difficult to detect. In fact, it passes right through the empty space between the particles which make up matter, and only collides with another particle on very rare occasions. It was not until 1956 when the neutrino was actually "seen" in a collision with another bit of solid matter that its existence could definitely be confirmed.

But it was this elusive quality which the neutrino possesses and the fact that it has no rest mass or electrical charge, which makes it possible for us to now "see" into the sun's interior and determine what is happening *right now.*

We know that neutrinos are produced in the fusion of hydrogen and we know just how many neutrinos result from the fusion of a given mass of hydrogen. Therefore it was a simple task to calculate just how many neutrinos the sun's nuclear furnace should be emitting per second and how many of these particles should be striking a square centimeter of the earth's surface each second, and the number is tremendous.

At this very instant, as you are reading this, billions of neutrinos are passing through you. Once in about ten years one of these particles will strike an atom in your body. Even if it is nighttime, the stream of solar neutrinos pass right through the earth and are zipping through you — from the floor of your room. Neutrinos may, in fact, be one of the most numerous sub-atomic particles in the entire universe.

An ingenious method of detecting and counting neutrinos was devised a number of years ago by Dr. Raymond Davis of the Brookhaven National Laboratory. When a neutrino collides with a chlorine atom, an atom of radioactive argon is produced. Argon, being a noble gas, does not react chemically with any other element. Being radioactive, Argon 37 may be accurately measured, down to the number of individual atoms, by radiation counters. This method was tested at the National Accelerator Laboratory and was found to work very well, measuring neutrinos with a high degree of accuracy.

Although the quantity of solar neutrinos had been calculated, they had never been measured. Dr. Davis decided to do just this. In order to make certain that other particles would not interact with the chlorine, the experiment was conducted deep inside the earth at the Homestake Mine at Lead, South Dakota. A tank containing 100,000 gallons of perchloroethylene was placed 4,800 feet down in the mine, along with the other equipment to measure the interaction of neutrinos with the chlorine and count the atoms of radioactive argon produced.

After several months, when a sufficient quantity of radio-active argon should have been produced, it was measured and the first evaluation of solar neutrinos was made. The results were disappointing. Not nearly enough neutrinos had been detected by the equipment.

The test was repeated and after several more months the radioactive argon was measured. Again the results did not coincide with the calculations. The equipment was checked and double checked, but nothing was found wrong with the equipment. The experiment was repeated again and again with the same results. Only twenty percent of the calculated neutrinos were found to be coming from our sun.

Finally the meaning of these results struck home. The sun was producing only about one-fifth as many neutrinos as it should be emitting. We were seeing right into the core of the sun, measuring not the million-year-old photons of light, but what was going on *right now*.

Either we did not really understand the solar nuclear fusion process, or *the sun was being shut down*.

The results of the neutrino detection experiments have caused physicists to perform all sorts of theoretical dances to explain them. The Homestake Mine apparatus has been measuring solar neutrinos long enough to have obtained records through two cyclic fluctuations. One of these is the eleven-year cycle of sunspots, where neutrino detection has been shown to be low when sunspot activity is high, and slightly higher when there is little sunspot activity.

The other cycle reported by Raymond Davis correlated with a variation caused by the earth's rotation around the sun, whose axis is inclined at 6 degrees. Davis has found that twice each year, on June 5 and December 5, the neutrinos are beamed to earth through the sun's equatorial region, where the magnetic field of the sun is lowest. His data indicates that during this period neutrino detection is decreased.

This is puzzling, however, for if neutrinos do have a small rest mass or magnetic moment, as some have suggested, the opposite effect would be expected.

A theoretical proposal, known as the Mikhaev-Smirnov-Wolfenstein (MSW) effect, in which magnetic interactions change neutrinos from one kind to another, has been accepted as a possible explanation of the discrepancy between the observed number of neutrinos and the calculated number. Three types of neutrinos are known to exist — the electron, the muon, and the tau neutrino, named for the other particle with which they are produced in nuclear reactions. The Homestake detectors are sensitive only to electron neutrinos. However, this theory which proposes that an electron neutrino can be transformed into another type in the tiny fraction of time it is contained within the sun, would force drastic changes in the understanding of particle physics involving neutrinos.

This has prompted a rash of laboratory experiments to determine whether or not the neutrino actually possesses a small rest mass. A few of these have claimed positive results, but the vast majority have indicated it has none. The entire neutrino situation has remained quite uncertain.

In other parts of the world neutrino detection equipment is being set up. Since 1987 the one located in Kamioka, Japan has been measuring solar neutrinos from a different nuclear process than the equipment at the Homestake Mine. Results from Kamiokande II, as reported by Yoji Tatsuka of the University of Tokyo, seem to confirm Raymond Davis' findings that the sun is producing far less neutrino flux than calculations predict that it should be producing.

Two additional installations using a different type of neutrino detection material are being constructed. With Raymond Davis' apparatus, huge quantities of chlorine are used and a neutrino in collision with a chlorine atom, Cl-37, produces an atom of radioactive argon, Ar-37, and an electron. But this type of reaction detects only high energy neutrinos. The two new installations will use gallium in place of chlorine and be able to detect neutrinos of much lower energy coming from the sun's interior. When an atom of gallium-71 absorbs a neutrino, it is transformed into an atom of radioactive germanium-71, which is then counted.

The joint Soviet-American gallium experiment (SAGE) at the Baksan underground laboratory in the mountainous North Caucasus region has reported its first data. Calculations indicate that SAGE should be picking up about one neutrino each day — if the sun is producing the quantity and type of neutrinos scientists predict it should.

The preliminary results from SAGE are shocking. In fact, no neutrinos other than what one would expect from a background count (those coming from stars other than the sun) have been detected. Since the gallium equipment is designed to measure low energy neutrinos — those resulting from the prime energy producing reactions within the sun's core — these results indicate that indeed either something is drastically wrong with the apparatus, *or something is drastically wrong with our sun!*

Another experiment is being set up using gallium at the Gran Sasso underground laboratory in the Apennine Mountains east of Rome, Italy. This has just begun operation, and if data there confirms the results from SAGE, scientists will be forced to admit that there are strange things happening in the star which provides our earth with the warmth, light, and energy that makes life possible on it.

But whatever the case, the fact is extremely clear that *something* is happening within our sun which scientists cannot now explain. They are looking for new and radical theories to attempt to circumvent this problem. But to the believing Christian, the facts of this matter should be no mystery at all.

Jesus said very plainly, "Immediately after the tribulation of those days shall the sun be darkened, and the moon shall not give her light" (Matt. 24:29).

He is quoted in Mark 13:24 as saying exactly the same thing. In Luke 21:25 Jesus foretold that there would be signs in the sun, the moon, and the stars just prior to His coming again in power and glory at the end of this age.

Jesus said it and I believe it! Now perhaps even scientists will begin to look elsewhere for an explanation of what is happening to the sun.

What are the consequences of the sun's solar furnace being turned down? What will happen to the sun and the earth if this is indeed true? Well, scientists have no dispute about that! It is the pressure exerted by the reactions within the sun's fusion furnace which counterbalance the sun's extreme gravity that tries to pull the ball of hydrogen gas toward its center. Without that outward pressure, the sun would collapse inward. This, scientists agree, would result in absolute catastrophe for the earth and the entire solar system.

The collapsing gas of the sun would heat the interior to billions of degrees within seconds. Suddenly the nuclear reactions would re-start — this time not in a steady release of heat and light — but with a cataclysmic explosion. The sun would expand rapidly and consume all of the nearby planets such as Mercury, Venus, Earth, and Mars in a fiery incinerator.

Our sun is not believed large enough to become a supernova. Stars about twice the mass of the sun, when they die, explode with an energy so great that they expel their gasses out into the infinite reaches of space as super-novas. It was from the remnants of one of these gigantic detonations, in which elements heavier than iron are produced, that our earth and perhaps our entire solar system was made in the day of our creation.

Should we, as Christians, be astonished at such an incendiary climax to the earth as we now know it? Not at all, for we are told exactly what to expect. In 2 Peter 3:10 we find the answer: "But the day of the Lord will come as a thief in the night; in the which the heavens shall pass away with a great noise, and the elements shall melt with fervent heat, the earth also and the works that are therein shall be burned up."

Without corroborative evidence it would be possible to explain away the discrepancy in calculated versus observed solar neutrinos, as many scientists have attempted to do, on the basis that the fusion reaction going on within the sun is somehow different than we believed it to be. If this were true, then the lesser quantities of neutrinos could be perfectly normal and nothing had "gone wrong" in the sun's core and we would have nothing to worry about. But other evidence has been found.

Jack Eddy and Aram Boornazian of the Harvard-Smithsonian National Center for Atmospheric Research have found that the diameter of the sun has been shrinking since at least 1853 when scientists were first able to measure it. This shrinkage appears to be at the rate of one-tenth percent per century, or about five feet per hour. This doesn't sound like much, considering the size of the sun, but if this rate were to continue, the diameter of the sun would be zero in only about 100,000 years. This, of course, runs counter to what scientists have told us about our star: that it would continue to shine as it does today for at least another five billion years. *Something* is happening to our sun, and the scientific community is at a loss to explain it.

The diameter of the sun will not reach zero. Long before that other events will occur to bring an end to life on this planet as we know it. Right now we are witnessing the fulfillment of many of the other signs which Jesus gave us to signal His coming again and the end of this age. We are the generation which is observing these signs, and Jesus also told us, "This generation shall not pass, till all these things be fulfilled" (Matt. 24:34).

I believe that twentieth century science is providing the evidence for what the Bible has told us to expect from our special star, the sun, and that exactly what Jesus said to watch for is happening right now.

Science is inadvertently confirming what the Bible has already told us. The Bible was not intended to be a scientific book. It is concerned with man's relationship with his Creator. But what God has chosen to tell us in the Bible about history, geography, politics, or science is true and accurate. There cannot possibly be any contradiction, as long as scientists have their facts straight and theologians do not read more into the Bible than it actually says.

But the truth is there as it has been for thousands of years. Perhaps now scientists will begin to realize that fact.

Author's Note

As this book was being prepared to go to press the awaited preliminary report was received from the GALLEX neutrino detectors at the underground laboratory at Gran Sasso, Italy.[5] Thomas J. Bowles of Los Alamos National Laboratory says, "This is the fourth solar neutrino experiment which has observed a deficit of neutrinos from the sun. Once again it has been confirmed that there is something unusual going on. The question now is what."

I would suggest that he look at Matthew 24:29 for the answer to his question.

22

What Happened to the Air That Jesus Breathed?

I heard someone say that once in our lives we are all likely to breathe in a molecule of the same air that Julius Caesar exhaled in his last, dying gasp. This caused me to think — not about the air that Julius Caesar might have breathed — but the air that our Lord Jesus Christ inhaled and exhaled while He was on this earth. What happened, I wondered, to that air? What is the probability of a person breathing some of that very same air today?

I did some calculations.

When I had completed them, I was astonished.

The Calculations

It was reasonably simple to calculate. What I needed to know was the average quantity of air an average person inhales in every breath, multiply this by the average respiration rate per minute, then by the number of hours, days, and years of Jesus' lifetime. Since we are told that He was in His thirties when He was crucified, I used thirty years as the basis of my calculations.

Each respiration averages 0.35 liters of air.
Average respiration rate is 12 per minute.
Liters per minute equals 4.2.
4.2 X 60 minutes/hr. X 24 hrs./day equals 6048 liters/day.
6048 liters/day X 365 days equals 2,153,088 liters/year.
In 30 years, 30 X 2,153,088 equals 64,592,640 liters of air.

I rounded this off and used mathematical shorthand for the zeroes and arrived at a figure of 6.5×10^7 liters of air that Jesus would have breathed in thirty years of His life on earth.

Now we must calculate how many *molecules* were in those 6.5×10^7 liters of air that He breathed. Using Avogadro's number, which states that in every 22.4 liters of *any* gas, there are 6×10^{23} molecules under standard conditions of 1 atmosphere pressure and 0° Centigrade temperature, we can arrive at the number of molecules of air that He breathed in thirty years.

Jesus certainly lived under 1 atmosphere of pressure, but not under 0° Centigrade average temperature, for that is the freezing point of water. I checked the average temperature of Palestine and found that I could use an average temperature of 25° Centigrade, or 77° Fahrenheit, and be reasonably close. When I corrected for this temperature difference, it was determined that 22.4 liters would contain 5×10^{23} molecules of air in Palestine during the life of Jesus.

When we use this in our calculation of the number of molecules of air that Jesus breathed in thirty years, we get:

$(6.5 \times 10^7) \times (5 \times 10^{23})/22.4$ equals 1.3×10^{30} molecules of air.

How Many Liters of Air Are in Our Atmosphere?

In the almost two thousand years since Jesus lived, I found that it was not unreasonable to assume that the air He breathed has now been completely mixed with the rest of the air in the atmosphere. Certainly the wind currents have dispersed these molecules far and wide. I do not think we would be wrong in assuming that they have been thoroughly integrated into the world's atmosphere.

Now we must calculate how many liters of air are in our atmosphere that the molecules of Jesus' breath have been mixed with. The air in our atmosphere is largely contained in the first ten miles above the earth. We can arrive at its volume by first calculating the earth's spherical volume, then the earth's plus ten additional miles, and subtracting.

Using the standard formula for calculating the volume of a sphere:

V_1 equals $4.189r^3$

And the radius of the earth as 3,963 miles, then:

V_1 equals $4.189 \times (3963)^3$

V_1 equals 260,724,930,000 cubic miles as the volume of the earth.

The volume of the earth plus the atmosphere would be:

V_2 equals $4.189 \times (3973)^3$

V_2 equals 262,703,610,000 cubic miles.

Subtracting $V_2 - V_1$ equals 1,978,680,000 cubic miles.

The volume of the atmosphere may be expressed as 2×10^9 cubic miles.

One cubic mile equals $(5280)^3$ feet, or 147,197,950,000 cubic feet.

Since 1 cu. ft. equals 28.3 liters, then 1 cubic mile equals: $28.3 \times 147,187,950,000$ or 4×10^{12} liters of air.

The entire atmosphere would contain (4×10^{12}) (2×10^9) or 8×10^{21} liters of air.

The Air We Breathe Today

Air contains about 21% oxygen, 78% nitrogen, 1% argon, and minute amounts of carbon dioxide, hydrogen, helium, krypton, and other gasses. Some of the oxygen we inhale is converted to carbon dioxide, which we exhale. This, in turn, is taken up by plants and trees and becomes part of the cycle of photosynthesis. A small amount of nitrogen in the air is "fixed" by certain bacteria into compounds used by vegetation.

Not all of the air that Jesus breathed would be available today; some of the carbon dioxide He exhaled would have been utilized by plant life or have dissolved in the ocean. A small amount of the nitrogen He breathed would have been converted into plant nutrients. How much would be still circulating in our air today? How many molecules of that very air would be dispersed in the air we breathe today?

I am going to use an *extremely* conservative figure of only 1%.

Molecules That Jesus Breathed Available Today

If we use a figure of only 1% of all the molecules of air that Jesus breathed being available today, we calculate the following:

0.01 X 1.3 X 10^{30} equals 1.3 X 10^{28} molecules.

When we divide that by the number of liters of air in today's atmosphere, we get:

1.3 X 10^{28}/8 X 10^{21} equals 1.6 X 10^{6}

This means that every liter of today's air contains 1,600,000 molecules of air that Jesus breathed during His lifetime on earth.

Since we breathe in about a third of a liter of air every time we inhale, we draw into our bodies over 500,000 of the same molecules of air that our Lord once breathed. A half million in every breath we take!

The Implication of This

In John 20:22 we are told that Jesus *breathed* on His disciples, saying, "Receive ye the Holy Ghost." This very same breath from Jesus is physically available to us today, in fact we draw it into our bodies with every breath we take.

When we speak, it is with a portion of the same air that He spoke with. When we pray, it is with some of the identical molecules of air that He prayed with. Truly, He abides within us, for within our bodies is *His very breath!*

Peter asks the question in 2 Peter 3:11: "What manner of persons ought ye to be in all holy conversation?" Peter may not have been aware that two thousand years later people would still be breathing the same air that the Lord had breathed, but it is a question each of us should ask ourselves.

If we are using *His* breath when we speak, then we should be very careful of what we say. It is a very sobering thing to consider that when we *lie*, it is with His very breath that we do it. When a person *curses*, it is with the same molecules of air that the Son of God breathed. We should be very careful, indeed!

The Bible tells us that God inhabits the praises of His people. This is even more true when we realize that we praise Him with His very own breath. Jesus told us in Matthew 28:20: "Lo, I am with you always, even unto the end of the world." Indeed He is, for within each one of us is His very breath.

23

Mysteries Science Cannot Explain

In the previous chapters of this book we examined many subjects in an attempt to better understand them in the light of science. We have used physics and chemistry, mathematics and archaeology, historical records and linguistics, astronomy and geology. We have found conclusive evidence that in each and every case what the Bible tells us is both historically accurate and scientifically verifiable.

But there are other events described in the Bible that science cannot explain. I believe that these must be taken on faith. Faith can be based on the fact that so much of Scripture, which *can* be verified, has been proven to be correct. If a person is traveling from San Francisco to New York, and the road map has successfully guided him all the way to the entrance to the Holland Tunnel, that person should have absolute confidence that it will also take him the few additional miles into New York City.

God is the author of truth, and this truth is found in His Word, the Bible. We have seen circumstances in which God has directed *natural* events to accomplish His will. Since He is the Creator of nature, and has ordained the laws which govern it, is it unreasonable to assume that He is also capable of *suspending* these laws if He so desires? Should we question the ability of the Creator and origin of life to *restore* that life to the dead? I think not!

The first miracle Jesus performed was at a wedding feast when the host was embarrassed because the wine was insufficient for the number of guests. Reluctantly, at the urging of Mary, He turned plain water into wine. Scientifically, this cannot be explained, but have we any right to doubt that this really happened?

On two occasions Jesus multiplied a few loaves of bread and a few fish into a sufficient quantity of food for thousands to eat and be satisfied. Again, there can be absolutely no scientific explanation of this event. It was truly a miracle — beyond the realm of man's intellect to comprehend. But to the God who first created these substances, it was a simple task indeed. Scripture tells us that with God "nothing is impossible."

Jesus instantly healed many people. The blind received sight, the lame suddenly found their limbs to be straight and strong, lepers were cleansed, and fevers disappeared immediately. On at least three occasions He restored the dead to life. Impossible? Not at all, for He is the source of life itself.

John 1:4 tells us about Jesus, "In him was life . . ." and in John 5:26 Jesus confirmed this: "For as the Father hath life in himself; so hath he given to the Son to have life in himself."

At the hill called Golgotha, Jesus was executed. He was dead, and there is scientific evidence that He was truly dead. Yet He arose from the grave *alive!* Certainly this cannot be scientifically explained, but this is the crux of our Christian faith. Unless a person believes in the Resurrection, he cannot claim to be a Christian.

The answer to how this was possible cannot be found in medical books, but in the truth of the words of Jesus. "Therefore doth my Father love me, because I lay down my life, that I might take it again. No man taketh it from me, but I lay it down of myself. I have power to lay it down, and I have power to take it again, This commandment have I received of my Father" (John 10:17-18).

If Jesus had the power to lay down His life and take it up again, which He did, then how can we question His power to perform the other miracles, which pale by comparison to the miracle of His Resurrection?

Perhaps the greatest mystery which we cannot explain is God's love for us that was so great that He sent His only Son to die in our place for *our* sins. Can you image any earthly judge in any court of law taking the place of the convicted defendant, and allowing *himself* to be executed in order to spare the life of that condemned person? Yet that is what the final and supreme judge of this world did. In the person of Jesus Christ, God offered himself as the ultimate sacrifice for our salvation.

God *can* do anything, but there is one circumstance in which He will not exercise His power. He will not *force* us to accept the sacrifice made by His Son. That decision is ours alone to make, and we must accept *by our own free will.*

When Lazarus had been in the tomb four days, Jesus went to Bethany. Martha, Lazarus' sister met Him and Jesus asked her a question which He asks to all men everywhere: "I am the resurrection and the life: he that believeth in me, though he were dead, yet shall he live: and whosoever liveth and believeth in me shall never die. Believest thou this?" (John 11:25).

Martha answered, "Yea, Lord, I believe that thou art the Christ, the Son of God."

If you have not already accepted the greatest offer ever made, do it now. Say, along with Martha, "Yea, Lord, I believe."

The decision is yours, and yours alone, to make. Jesus told us that He had come so that we might have life and have it more abundantly, here and for all eternity.

Choose life!

Accept His sacrifice, made for you!

If you have not already done so, do it now!

Tomorrow may be too late!

Notes

Chapter 1

[1]P.J. Wiseman, *Ancient Records and the Structure of Genesis* (Nashville, TN: Thomas Nelson, 1985).

Chapter 2

[1]Books by Ivan Panin are available from J.S. Bentley, Bible Numerics, 7600 Jubilee Drive, Niagara Falls, Ont. Canada L2G 7J6.

Chapter 3

[1]J.C. Dillow, *The Waters Above* (Chicago, IL: Moody Press, 1981).

[2]Larry Vardiman, *The Sky Has Fallen* (Pittsburgh, PA: Proceedings of the First International Conference on Creationism, 1986).

[3]C.H. Kang and Ethel Nelson, *The Discovery of Genesis* (St. Louis, MO: Concordia Publishing Co., 1979).

[4]J.C. Whitcomb and H.M. Morris, *The Genesis Flood* (Phillipsburg, NJ: Presbyterian and Reformed Publishing Co., 1970).

[5]Walter T. Brown, *The Fountains of the Great Deep* (Pittsburgh, PA: Proceedings of the First International Conference on Creationism, 1986).

Chapter 4

[1]Merrill F. Unger, *Unger's Bible Handbook* (Chicago, IL: Moody Press, 1966), p. 896.

[2]Flavius Josephus, *Antiquities of the Jews* (Grand Rapids, MI: Kregel Publications, 1978), Book VI, IX, 1.

Chapter 10

[1]Brian M. Fagan, *The Journey from Eden* (New York, NY: Thames and Hudson, 1990), p. 25-30.

[2]James Shreeve, "Argument Over a Woman: Science Searches for the Mother of Us All," *Discover Magazine*, Vol. 11, Num. 8, August 1990.

[3]James Shreeve, "Origins Watch: Madam, I'm Adam," *Discover Magazine*, Vol. 12, Num. 6, June 1991.

[4]Michael H. Brown, *The Search for Eve* (San Francisco, CA: Harper & Row, 1990), p. 298.

Chapter 12

[1]Keller, *The Bible as History*, p. 130.

Chapter 13

[1]Keller, *The Bible as History*, p. 168.

[2]*Webster's New World Dictionary*, Second College Edition (New York, NY: Simon and Schuster, 1979).

Chapter 14

[1]Charles Warren, *Underground Jerusalem* (London: Richard Bentley & Sons, 1876), p.164-189.

[2]Ernst Sellin and Carl Watzinger, *Jericho* (Leipzig: J.C. Hinrichs, 1913).

[3]John Garstang and J.B.E. Garstang, *The Story of Jericho*, Revised Edition (London: Marshall, Morgan and Scott, 1948).

[4]John Garstang, "Jericho and the Biblical Story," *Wonders of the Past*, edited by J.A. Hammerton (New York, NY: Wise, 1937), p. 1222.

[5]Kathleen Kenyon, "Excavations at Jericho 1952," Palestine Excavations Quarterly, 1952, p. 4-6; "Excavations at Jericho 1957-58," Palestine Excavations Quarterly, 1960, p. 88-113, (London : British School of Archaeology in Jerusalem).

[6]Kathleen Kenyon, "Jericho," *Archaeology and Old Testament Study*, edited by D. Winton Thomas (Oxford: Clarendon, 1967), p. 265-267.

[7]Kathleen Kenyon, *Excavations at Jericho, Voume 5*, (London: British School of Archaeology in Jerusalem, 1983).

[8]Kenyon, *Excavations at Jericho, Volume 3*, (London: British School of Archaeology in Jerusalem, 1981).

[9]Bryant G. Wood, "Did the Israelites Conquer Jericho? A New Look at Archaeological Evidence," *Biblical Archaeology Review*, Vol. XVI, No. 2, March/April 1990.

[10]Ibid.

[11]Amos Nur, quoted in *The Stanford Observer*, November 1988.

Chapter 16

[1]Merrill C. Tenney and William White, Jr., *The Bible Almanac* edited by James I. Packer (Nashville, TN: Thomas Nelson Publishers, 1980), p. 25.

[2]Ibid.

[3]Josephus, *Antiquities*, Book I, VI, 4.

[4]Tenney and White, *The Bible Almanac*, p. 205.

[5]Keller, *The Bible as History*, p. 85

Chapter 17

[1]Unger, *Bible Handbook*, p. 415.

[2]Tenney and White, *The Bible Almanac*, p. 237.

[3]Ibid.

Chapter 18

[1]Josephus, *Antiquities*, Book VI, VIII, 4,5.

[2]Josephus, *The Wars of the Jews*, Book VI, IV, 8.

Chapter 20

[1]Dr. Michio Kaku and Jennifer Trainer, *Beyond Einstein* (New York, NY: Bantam Books, 1987), p. 4, 105, 124-128, 131.

[2]Frank Close, Michael Martin, and Christine Sutton, *The Particle Explosion* (New York, NY: Oxford University Press, 1987), p. 214-215.

[3]Gary Taubes, "Everything's Now Tied to Strings," *Discover Magazine*, Vol. 7, Num. 11, November 1986.

[4]Jeremy Bernstein, *The Tenth Dimension* (New York, NY: McGraw-Hill Publishing Co., 1989), p. 153.

Chapter 21

[1]John N. Bahcall, "Neutrinos from the Sun," *Frontiers in Astronomy* (San Francisco, CA: W.H. Freeman and Company, 1970), p. 108 ff.

[2]D.E. Thomsen, "Solar Neutrino Mysteries Persist," *Science News*, Vol. 133, April 30, 1988.

[3]"Serious Shortfall of Solar Neutrinos," *Science News*, Vol. 138, September 1, 1990.

[4]David W. Dunham et al, "Observations of a Probable Change in the Solar Radius Between 1715 and 1979," *Science*, Vol. 210, December 12, 1980.

[5]Ivars Peterson, "At Last, Neutrino Results from Gallex," *Science News*, Vol. 141, June 13, 1992.